Light on the Horizon

The Joy and Challenge of Real Ideas

by Kelly Richard Nicholson

Dr. Nicholson is available for motivational speaking engagements, business conferences, courses, lectures, and seminars. Contact the publishing company listed below or send e-mail to Kr7arjuna@aol.com.

First Edition 1999

Library of Congress Catalog Card Number: 99-90130
ISBN 0-9668911-0-4

Light on the Horizon: *The Joy and Challenge of Real Ideas*

Homeward Bound Publishing, Inc.
P. O. Box 1468 • 499 East Parowan Way • Draper, UT 84020
Toll Free 1-888-433-1130 • Fax (801) 816-1170

e-mail: homewardpb@aol.com

website: www.need2read.com

Printed in the United States of America

Illustrations by Brad Lee Wolverton

Cover design by Ranée Stam

Cover Photo by Karen Johnson

Don't just say you have read books. Show that through them you have learned to think better, to be a more discriminating and reflective person. Books are the training weights of the mind.

Epictetus, *The Art of Living*

... to myself I seem to have been only like a boy, playing on the seashore ... (see chapter 4)

Contents

List of Illustrations

Introduction

There are certain ideas at the heart of life. They are core ideas, vital and basic, that provide the ground of our thought and activity. Included in their number are *truth*, *freedom*, *value*, and *rationality*. They are essential to who we are and to how we live.

What manner of ideas are these? Surely they are not new. But they are current. They are, one might say, prime factors of our experience, themes inherent in our life drama. In Athens the marketplace rang loud with them. Today, lifestyle and intellectual landscape have changed, but these ideas remain.

And arguments over them continue. We live in an age when topics like value and conduct are open to discussion as never before. Recent decades have seen an upheaval of tradition; in the wake is a flash-flood of programs offering guidance. Yet for all of this interest in a good life, there is little interest, it seems, in any truth or principle that might provide its basis. At present there is much skepticism, much doubt as to whether or not real answers exist, let alone where they reside. One man's truth, it seems, is another's lie; values are merely "relative."

This skepticism is nothing new. Man, said the ancient sophist Protagoras, "is the measure of all things."[1] Truth and falsehood vary, in other words, with each observer: What is good, what is beautiful, lies not in *fact*, but in *perception*. Justice, said one contemporary, is but "the interest of the stronger" - a mind-set instilled into citizens in order to serve the interests of their rulers.[2]

This attitude prevails today. So much so, it seems, that few people have any sense of an alternative. But there is an alternative, a crucially different way to understand our place and calling. Truth, by its estimate, is real; value exists, and it issues a demand. The universe, by the same token, is not some dark and empty cosmic dance. It is a drama invested with worth and meaning.

This view has its own long history.[3] It is, say some, the timeless view, the one voicing in every age the song of the human spirit. To such a view this book is devoted. In

---

[1] See, for example, Plato's dialogue *Theatetus* 152a and following. This work is contained in Edith Hamilton and Huntington Cairns, eds., *The Collected Dialogues of Plato* (Princeton, New Jersey: Princeton University Press, 1973). For discussion of the sophists and their views, see W. K. C. Guthrie, *The Sophists* (Cambridge: Cambridge University Press, 1971).

[2] This famous definition is offered by Thrasymachus in Plato's *Republic*, chapter I, 338c. See again Hamilton and Cairns.

[3] For a classic discussion see Part I of C. S. Lewis' *The Abolition of Man* (New York: Simon and Schuster, 1996). This book had its first printing in 1944.

its pages the reader will find expressions of this timeless alternative. There are, said Socrates, real answers to life's questions, and it is our business to know them. The indwelling view of this book is that Socrates was right - that inquiry into truth is essential to a life well-lived. Life, on this view, has objective meaning. It has a direction and a purpose.[4]

Kindred voices speak to us through the ages. If we today desire a sense of who we are, of what it means to enlighten or actualize ourselves, we might listen. Insight into the human condition goes far back, and it finds expression in many neighborhoods. The scope of this work is accordingly wide. But the discussion is not all-accepting. As to truth, it advocates no democracy. Its keystone is not trend or popularity, but something more; it seeks for what is real, what is absolute, for the reality that bestows upon life an essential rightness.

This book is intended to stir the reader's reflection. It is intended also to stimulate active change. For there is a difference between musing over a piece of literature and absorbing one. There is a difference likewise between thought and action. If we are to gain from a book, we must do more than look at it; we must read not only with the mind, but with the will.

---

[4] See, for example, *Apology* 38a. (Hamilton and Cairns)

Laid out in this work are ten theme-chapters central to human experience. The first two concern practical issues of life conduct and personal development. The third discusses the popular and longstanding ideal of heroism. In the next three chapters come somewhat more abstract issues concerning truth, value, and the nature of human agency. These focus upon such things as the nature of reason, the status of moral value, and the question of free will. Chapter 7 examines the ideal of beauty. The final three chapters extend this investigation beyond the limits of the present world.

This book seeks for a truth behind appearances. To what end? The enterprise, thinks Plato, has an inherent reward. For in attempting it, we will be better and wiser than we might have been. Philosophy aids us, in this present round, while it reveals to us, in the process, life's greater meaning. Its voyage is the voyage of the soul. By its light we are led home. We apprehend our own higher direction and the union, at last, of all truth and goodness. In this spirit we are bid to set sail.

I

The Conduct of Life

This chapter, as its title suggests, has to do with issues of personal character and the broad strategy of life conduct. What attitudes, what policies of behavior, make for ultimate success in the life enterprise? The following discussion addresses such themes as courage, honesty, forthrightness, and personal faith as daily operating principles.

Honesty

> The quest for honesty is not like a search for a jewel that may end happily with the attainment of what is wanted. It is rather like the quest for excellence, a prolonged struggle.
>
> Walter Kaufmann, *The Faith of a Heretic*

Honesty. The word is not harsh or confronting. It stands before us in quiet challenge. It poses a lifetime task.

Honesty, writes Walter Kaufmann, is a quest.[1] Thus it is not a place at which we arrive, once and for all time. There are few things, he adds, about which we are less honest than honesty itself.

The task of honesty, Kaufmann observes, is more subtle than we may first realize. A high level of honesty requires not just an allegiance to basic rules, but an exercise of imagination. It requires a respect for truth that goes beyond issues of lying or gross manipulation. "There are degrees of honesty," Kaufmann writes, "no less than of courage or humility."

---

[1] Walter Kaufmann, *The Faith of a Heretic* (New York: Doubleday and Co., 1961).

Honesty, like courage, has varieties. It has physical and moral dimensions. A fair number of men, it has been said, will stand up to their enemies, while few, by contrast, will stand up to their friends. Thus there are some individuals, for example, who will not flinch at physical danger, but who will fail to stand by an ideal when it will cost something. It is one thing to face outright confrontation; it is another, says Kaufmann, to remain true to oneself, choosing integrity over material advantage.

Physical honesty, in the same vein, is a simple thing. It involves merely an abstinence from gross deceit. Moral honesty, extending this comparison, requires a fineness of character, a capacity to see our own ideas, our own convictions, from new points of view. It means a receptivity to criticism. It is a triumph over self-deceit.

A high level of honesty involves an appreciation of what honesty itself involves. Instead of asking whether you are honest or not, says Kaufmann, ask *how you could become more honest*. You do this, he explains, by developing *intellectual imagination* - "carefulness, conscientiousness, scrupulousness - by making your beliefs and statements matters of conscience."[2]

---

[2] *Ibid.*, p. 39.

The Will to Believe

> Indeed we *may* wait if we will ... but if we do so, we do so at our peril as much as if we believed. In either case we *act*, taking our life in our hands.
>
> William James, "The Will to Believe"

Honesty might well be defined as *a respect for truth*. How does this respect bear upon ultimate questions? What is its relation to questions about our own greater destiny?

Faith, say some, is compromise. They think, writes William James, in the manner of the schoolboy who said, "Faith is when you believe something that you know ain't true." Religious folk, they imagine, lack integrity.

This view, as James observes, is expressed by W. K. Clifford in his essay "The Ethics of Belief". It is, writes Clifford, "wrong always, everywhere, and for anyone, to believe anything upon insufficient evidence."[3] Our beliefs do not affect merely ourselves. Others may depend on them. As a point of logic and moral policy, therefore, each belief should be as strong or weak as justification allows.

---

[3] W. K. Clifford, "The Ethics of Belief", contained in Burton F. Porter, ed., *Religion and Reason* (New York: St. Martin's Press, 1993), p. 199.

There are times, to be sure, when Clifford's formula applies. (He himself cites the case of a shipowner who convinces himself, at the cost of many lives, that his ship is adequate to complete a mission though it is old and worn.) But is it valid always? There are cases, thinks James, where a leap of faith, though it exceeds the bounds of evidence, is legitimate. For there are times, he explains, when this leap may yield truth.

Take the case of friendship. "Do you like me or not?" The answer to this question, says James, depends often on whether or not I am willing to meet you half-way. Similarly, says James, with romance: "How many women's hearts are vanquished," he asks, "by the mere sanguine insistence of some man that they *must* love him!" Fact and feeling may bear upon one another.

In such cases, my willingness to believe has a rational basis. For it may enable me to discover something that would have remained hidden otherwise. Indeed my attitude may have *an active bearing on the fact itself*. It may shape the situation, may create facts different from the ones that would hold otherwise. In such a case this optimism may be a help and not a hindrance. Hence faith is sometimes aligned with rationality.

So it may be with religion. To think of the universe in religious terms, says James, is to think of it more as a

Thou than as an *It*, more like consciousness than like an object. Perhaps not everyone can accept this hypothesis. There are some types, it is true, who cannot fathom another world, who cannot entertain the thought that reality may extend outside the bounds of the senses. But for those who find it plausible, who count it logically alive, this consideration is vital.

What is the substance of religious belief? Science, as James puts it, says that things are; morality says some things are better than others. Religion says essentially two things: The first is that "the best things are the more eternal things, the overlapping things, the things in the universe that throw the last stone, so to speak, and say the final word."[4] The second is that we are better off, even now, if we believe this to be true.

The *best* things are eternal: This is no mere flight of phrase or feeling. Saying that the best things are eternal means that eternity is what matters. We ourselves partake of it; we are more than mortal flesh, and our destiny is not confined to this world. Saying that the best things are eternal means that we are meant for more than present appearances disclose. The real life, the true investment, lies not here but in the greater spiritual scheme.

---

[4] William James, "The Will to Believe", contained in James' *The Will to Believe and other essays in popular philosophy* (New York: Dover Books, 1956), p. 25.

Believe truth! Shun error! We imagine, says James, that these are two sides of the same coin. But not always. At times they are at odds. The requirement that we avoid false assumption at all costs, as we have seen, can sometimes impose a limit upon our understanding. Excess caution in friendship, for example, may avoid error, but it may also avoid discovery. Perhaps it is the same in regard to the final truths of life. It may deny us what could be ours, were we willing to take the risk. If skepticism costs us the truth, it is not in the service of reason.

James' observation concerning the efficacy of belief is expressed once more in his kindred essay "Is Life Worth Living?".[5] Here again, we are reminded, the attitude of trust, of expectation, can make the difference. Believe that life is worth living, says James, and your attitude will help to create the fact. Defeat is not merely something that happens to you. It is in some measure your own doing. The question of whether or not life is worth living, of whether or not victory shall be yours, is not solved merely by estimate, but by choice. Belief has power. It can shape the world in which you live. For this reason you are justified, as a point of logic, in taking a willful approach to it.

---

[5] See this essay contained within the volume noted above.

Self and Others

> Essentially, getting people to like you is merely the other side of liking them.
>
> Norman Vincent Peale,
> *The Power of Positive Thinking*

About thirty years ago, when in my teens, I poured over the works of men like Norman Vincent Peale and Dale Carnegie. These authors, it seemed, were not just writers, but allies, kindred souls with life-blood in their words. We need not bow, they said, to circumstance. A change of attitude begins a revolution.

How to Win Friends and Influence People - the title of Carnegie's 1936 classic is a cliche to modern ears.[6] Practically everyone has heard of this volume. Few by comparison have read it,[7] or grasp its main ideas. It has to do not just with salesmanship, but with self-development. It is dedicated to the proposition that change in oneself can remake an entire life.

---

[6] Dale Carnegie, *How to Win Friends and Influence People* (New York: Simon and Schuster, 1982).

[7] It is a book of lessons in "manipulation," explained more than one professor of my undergraduate years, fully in keeping with the cynical fashion of the day.

One of the book's subdivisions is entitled "Six Ways to Make People Like You". The first of these ways is *Become Genuinely Interested in Other People*. Carnegie recalls the case of a magazine editor who visited his class at New York University and revealed a secret about successful writing. "If the author doesn't like people," explained this man, "people won't like his or her stories."[8]

If this is true of writing fiction, Carnegie continues, it applies as well to direct encounter. He describes a visit with magician Howard Thurston, who traveled the world for forty years, amazing audiences with his repertoire of act and illusion. What, asked Carnegie, was the secret of his success? Surely it lay not in his schooling, for this man had run away from home as a small boy. Thurston had spent his early years riding in boxcars, sleeping in haystacks, and begging for food from one door to the next. He had learned to read by looking out of train cars at signs along the way.

It did not lie, either, in his superior knowledge of magic. Hundreds of books, Thurston admitted, had been written on the subject by individuals who knew as much about the craft as he did. But he had, explains Carnegie, two things that made him unusual. First, he had showmanship, an ability to connect with his audience

---

[8] *Ibid.*, p. 55.

honed by endless rehearsal of every look and gesture that figured into the presentation. Second, he had an interest in people. In this Thurston was unlike other performers, who tended, as he put it, to look upon their audiences as being "hicks" and "suckers" to be bilked out of their money. He, by contrast, took the stage with a heartfelt gratitude toward these people who made his living possible and who deserved the best that he could give them.

Carnegie relates a number of stories showing how an interest in others can make the difference with respect to the success of an enterprise. Once, he recalls, he was teaching a course on fiction writing at the Brooklyn Institute of Arts and Sciences. He and his students hoped to persuade a number of busy authors to visit the campus and tell of their experiences in the field. How might such individuals be convinced that the project was worthwhile?

They wrote to each of them, recalls Carnegie, telling of their admiration and hoping to gain the benefit of the author's wisdom. Each letter was signed by about a hundred and fifty students. It acknowledged that the author was doubtless too busy to prepare a lecture, and offered instead a set of questions for him or her to answer about himself and his method of work. Who, asks Carnegie, would not find such an invitation agreeable? The method was a resounding success.

There are many times, it seems, when even an extra bit of effort is telling. The Duke of Windsor, Carnegie recalls, was a conscientious individual who spent months of study prior to his tour of South America so that he could address his audiences in their native tongue. He also minded details. For years, this man made it a point to find out the birthdays of his friends. He would begin by asking some innocuous question about whether or not the date of one's birth might have anything to do with one's character and disposition. Once getting this individual's date of birth, he repeated it to himself - "November 24, November 24" - until he could enter it into a book. At the beginning of a year, he would have all such dates noted to make sure that the letter or telegram was there on time. "What a hit it made!" he recalls. "I was frequently the only person on earth who remembered."[9]

Many, says Carnegie, have gained insights and solved problems by taking slight pains for those around them. He recalls the case of a man named Charles Walters who was assigned by the bank where he worked to prepare a detailed report on a corporation.

On entering the president's office, explained Walters, he learned that this executive had a son who collected unusual stamps. Getting nowhere in the interview, he

---

[9] *Ibid.*, p. 61.

returned the next afternoon and told the secretary that he had a wealth of stamps that had been received by the foreign department of his bank. The relationship between Walters and the president took a dramatic turn for the better, and Walters had more information than he needed without even asking for it.

Once a man named C. M. Knaphle described, in a speech in one of Carnegie's own classes, his bitter frustration at being unable to sell fuel to a certain chain store with a location in his neighborhoods. Knaphle, recalls Carnegie, poured out his wrath upon chain stores, deeming them to be a curse to the nation. Carnegie suggested that he try a different approach, and in the process set up a debate within the class concerning the effect of chain stores upon the nation. Knaphle himself was assigned to defend the chain as an institution! He went to the executive of the store that had been the cause of his frustration and asked for relevant information to support his side of the argument.

What happened next astounded him. Having asked for one minute of the man's time, he received nearly two hours. He left with all of the information and leads that he could manage. His attitude was completely changed. On leaving the office, Knaphle was asked to stay in contact, and to return for a fuel order when the time came.

It was, thought Knaphle, a miracle. "Here he was offering to buy fuel without my even suggesting it. I had made more headway in two hours by becoming genuinely interested in him and his problems than I could have made in ten years trying to get him interested in me and my product."[10]

There are some who disparage such lessons. Carnegie, they say, puts success ahead of sincerity. But surely such criticism misses the point. For the lesson of these examples is not mere flattery or technique. What they reveal is that real success, be it in sales, management, instruction, or many other things, involves *a sincere interest in the world outside oneself*. Someone who inherited ten million dollars would gain little if unable to see its application beyond self-amusement. It is a *genuine* interest in the world that makes the difference.

Kindred lessons abound in the writing of Norman Vincent Peale, whose time-honored work *The Power of Positive Thinking* is a classic of inspiration. While studies cite many traits important to popularity, there is one, he notes, at the center: "a sincere and forthright interest in and love for people."[11]

---

[10] *Ibid.*, p. 64.

[11] Norman Vincent Peale, *The Power of Positive Thinking* (New York: Ballantine, 1992), p. 194.

This requires integrity. It requires a willingness to find and uproot certain blocks within oneself that now impede success. Peale discusses, in this connection, the need to build the self-esteem of other persons. "If I deflate your ego and therefore your self-importance," he explains, "though you may laugh it off, I have deeply wounded you. In fact, I have shown disrespect for you, and while you may exercise charity toward me, even so, unless you are finely developed spiritually, you are not going to like me very well."

What we need, thinks Peale, is a largeness of mind and soul that allows us to give to others and to take joy in the fact. "Whomever you help to build up and become a better, stronger, finer person," he observes, "will give you his undying devotion." Do this, he adds, because you like them.

What Peale thus advocates is the cultivation of generosity. He lists a set of practical rules of interaction that lead in this direction. Thus it is good, for example, to remember people's names. It is also good to possess a natural humility. Never miss a chance, says Peale, to extend congratulations or sympathy when appropriate. Cultivate a strength that you can offer to others when it is needed, so that you can help them to be better and stronger persons themselves.

Modesty

> The silly vice of profanity illustrates the monotony of sin. Men begin to swear as an enrichment of the vocabulary. But nothing so contracts and impoverishes human speech.
>
> Robert Elliott Speer, *The Marks of a Man*

Perhaps no culture has comprehensive insight into the elements of human virtue. Over time such insight waxes and wanes, fading in one era and gaining revival in another. There are some virtues, it seems, in short supply at the present time. One of these is the cultivation of wholesome speech.

There has come a pivotal change in recent history. In this time an older way has been lost, and a new "freedom" has taken its place. I myself, to add a personal note, was in high school in the late 1960's when this wave reached its crest. Like many, I applauded its challenge of standing assumptions regarding value, lifestyle, and the old patriotism. And yet I could not manage a whole-hearted enthusiasm for this movement. Its sound, its gloat, its smug advocacy of drugs, promiscuity, and violent "protest" against police officers on campus - at its heart, I sensed, was an impulse not to justice, but to ruin.

One casualty of the era was self-restraint. Another and kindred loss was that of personal modesty. It was no longer thought worthwhile, for instance, to maintain a sense of tact or propriety in public situations. The abstinence from crude or vulgar expression was regarded as false inhibition.

What this attitude failed to grasp was that modesty is not simply a veneer. Its point is not to mask feeling. Public modesty is a reflection of inward decency. Vulgar speech, by contrast, is violation. It expresses a baseness not merely of word, but of sensibility. Modesty expresses personal elegance.

If modesty was a casualty of the 60's, it has fared little better in the time since, as confrontation and public embarrassment become mass entertainment staples and "in your face" attitude receives celebration. But again, the issue is not recent. It is part and parcel of human society. Character, writes Samuel Smiles, "exhibits itself in self-control of speech as much as in any thing else."[12] The profane man, says Robert Speer, imagines that his profanity is an enrichment.[13] It is instead the very

---

[12] Samuel Smiles, *Character* (New York: Harper and Brothers, Publishers, 1872), p. 177.

[13] Robert Elliot Speer, *The Marks of a Man* (Cincinnati: Jennings and Graham, 1907). See especially chapter 2, "Purity".

opposite. Such a man becomes the slave of these same few oaths that he chooses. Soon, by way of habit, all his emotion, all his intellect, must find its way through this strangled outlet. The result is a contraction of the soul.

We may go back further. One of the clearest marks of the moral life, insists the ancient stoic Epictetus, is right speech.[14] Our impulse is to give voice to each passing thought or feeling. In so doing we become trivial by habit. We need not be serious at every moment, but when the conversation is decaying, we should try to uplift it. Nor should we think that humor means vulgarity or malice. "Laugh *with*," says this Roman philosopher, but never *at*."

This advice finds a parallel in the teachings of the Buddha, who makes "right speech" a part of his Eightfold Path[15] of salvation. This man, as every student of world religions is told, announces four cosmic truths that summarize the human condition. The first of these is that life here is *dukkha*, a basic dis-ease or unsatisfactoriness.[16]

---

[14] Epictetus, *The Art of Living* (San Francisco: HarperCollins, 1995), p. 51. Sharon Lebell, editor.

[15] The eight are: Right understanding, right thought, right speech, right action, right livelihood, right effort, right mindfulness, and right concentration.

[16] While this Pali term is often translated as "pain" or "suffering," it might just as well be rendered as "dislocation." Yet our best moments here, the Buddha maintains, have inherent limits. The Eightfold Path is our escape from limitation altogether. See, for example, Walpola Rahula, *What the Buddha Taught* (New York: Grove Weidenfeld, 1974).

The second is that this fact has a cause, namely an egoistic craving or thirst that keeps us bound to this realm (and successive rebirth) by our own action. The third is that there exists an escape from this cycle. The fourth is the life-path that leads to liberation.

Like other elements of this path, right speech is a lifetime project. It involves not merely abstaining from lies, but from all slanderous, unpleasant, and mean-minded habits that cause harm. It means refraining likewise from speech that is harsh, impolite, or abusive, and from small talk or gossip that is idle and useless. Taken to heart, it thus becomes a discipline of the soul as well as the voice.

The Most Fundamental Law in All of Life

> All things are double, one against another. - Tit for tat, an eye for an eye, a tooth for a tooth; blood for blood; measure for measure; love for love. - Give and it shall be given you. - He that watereth shall be watered himself. - What will you have? Quoth God; pay for it and take it. - Nothing venture, nothing have.
>
> Ralph Emerson, "Compensation"

It is an idea that finds expression in a common phrase: You get what you pay for. Or, as is said endlessly in recent years, what goes around, comes around.

Many of us cite these old saws. Seldom do we stop to think about how much is in them. For no sooner do we offer them up than we betray them by seeking some prize - friendship, a college credit, a sexual favor, an enhanced reputation - by shading the truth.

There is, thinks Ralph Emerson, a justice working itself out in all that we do. Man, he writes, is a Providence to himself, dispensing good to his own goodness and evil to his own sin. "Thefts never enrich; alms, never impoverish; murder will speak out of stone walls." Thus the least compromise, the slightest admixture of lie or vanity, the least attempt to create a false impression, "will instantly vitiate the effect."[17]

The truly world-wise, he observes, will pay as they go. Does an individual gain by receiving a hundred favors and rendering none, by taking, "through indolence or cunning, his neighbor's wares, or horses, or money"? From such action arises "the instant acknowledgment of benefit on the one part, and of debt on the other." This fact remains in the mind of each, giver and borrower, and it colors every interaction thereafter. It cannot be erased without payment. Thus it will occur to the borrower in time that "he had better have broken his own bones than to have ridden in his neighbor's coach."

Some will read these words and nod in agreement. They will think that borrowing money is unwise, and that failing to repay it is worse. But there is more to the lesson than this. A wise man, says Emerson, will extend it everywhere. This principle of repayment concerns not just formal transaction, but every expenditure of energy, great or small, conspicuous or not, in a lifetime.

---

[17] Ralph Emerson, "An Address", contained in *The Selected Writings of Ralph Waldo Emerson*, ed. Brooks Atkinson (New York: The Modern Library, 1992), p. 65. As the editor notes, Emerson gave this address to the Harvard Divinity School in 1838. The freeness with which he invoked God and ultimate truth were a scandal, and nearly thirty years would pass before Emerson would receive another invitation from the college.

It is the certain balance of *Give* and *Take*, "the doctrine that everything has its price."[18] If the price is not paid, then nothing good will be forthcoming. It is a doctrine that has its examples in the budgets of states, the laws of light and darkness, and all the action and reaction of nature. "Put God in your debt," says Emerson. "Every stroke shall be repaid."[19]

This justice, he insists, applies across the board. You will not bring away from any conversation more than your mind is ready to acquire. Nor will you gain from company for which you are unworthy. Introduce a base man among gentlemen, and you see that he is not with them "even though his body is in the room."[20] No one can gain what he has not prepared himself to gain. God screens us from premature ideas. The soul is like fire; it "publishes its word through action, word, and countenance." "Pretension," Emerson insists, "never wrote an *Iliad*, nor drove back Xerxes." Its reward is sham.

---

[18] Emerson, "Compensation", contained in *Selected Writings*, p. 165.

[19] *Ibid.*, p. 167.

[20] See Emerson's "Ethics", contained in *Ralph Waldo Emerson - Selected Essays, Lectures, and Poems*, ed. Robert D. Richardson, Jr. (New York: Bantam Books, 1990), p. 74.

Veteran observers said that he had more God-given talent than any player they had seen.

II

Personal Growth

An industry has developed in recent years around the subject of personal growth and fulfillment. Success, self-realization, the distinction between ego and true selfhood - books and seminars abound. It is, of course, an old subject, perhaps as ancient as the race itself. Some of its best treatment is found likewise in times past. In Plato, Lao Tzu, and others we learn something of what is involved in personal development and in worthwhile human interaction. This chapter offers a miscellany of insight old and recent.

Truth and Ego

He who stands on tiptoe, does not stand firm.

Lao Tzu, *Tao te Ching*

He was, by all accounts, a curiosity. What we have on Lao Tzu today, observes Huston Smith,[1] is a mosaic of legend.

We hear often of this man's "enigmatic impression" and his fathomless depths. The venerable Confucius, it is said, once paid him a visit. "I know," he was heard to remark afterward,

> a bird can fly; I know a fish can swim; I know animals can run. Creatures that run can be caught in nets; those that swim can be caught in wicker traps; those that fly can be hit by arrows. But the dragon is beyond my knowledge; it ascends into heaven on the clouds and the wind. Today I have seen Lao Tzu, and he is like the dragon![2]

---

[1] Huston Smith, *The World's Religions* (San Francisco: HarperCollins, 1991). See chapter 5. See also Arthur Waley's classic text and commentary in *The Way and Its Power* (New York: Grove Weidenfeld, 1958). The quoted passage is from Waley's translation, chapter 24.

[2] *Ibid.*, pp. 196-97.

In time, it is written, when up in years and disillusioned with society, Lao Tzu climbed onto a water buffalo and rode west toward Tibet. At the Hankao Pass, a gatekeeper asked him to provide a record of his thoughts for the civilization he was leaving behind. The old master assented. He came back in three days with a slender volume. It numbered some five thousand characters and was entitled *Tao te Ching*, or *The Way and Its Power*. It can, says Smith, be read "in half an hour or a lifetime," and it remains to this day the basic text of Taoist thought.

He who stands on tiptoe does not stand firm. In trying to be more than we are, we insure our own failure. Falsehood and success are incompatible. Our need to perform, to look better or more sophisticated, turns our efforts to self-mockery. Those most worth impressing will be impressed the least.

No good comes from deceit. Even if we succeed in creating a false impression, we undermine ourselves. By means of this impression, we create false expectation, which brings further problems. An effort at misrepresentation is invariably an effort in the wrong direction.

This wisdom finds kindred expression in every age. False contemplatives, writes the anonymous author of the medieval classic *The Cloud of Unknowing*, "are more anxious to *appear* holy before men than to *be* holy before God and his angels."[3] Such types may cultivate the appearance of genuine mystics. They may gain reputation; they may find a following. But in the end, self-centeredness will pervert their spiritual exercises and lead them into darkness.

"True worth," writes Alice Cary, "is in *being*, not *seeming*."[4] The same applies to success. Ego is an obstacle. If we would write, if we would teach, if we would influence, we must begin by emptying ourselves of self-flattery. Our intentions must be constructive.

---

[3] See William Johnston, ed., *The Cloud of Unknowing* (New York: Image Books, 1996), p. 118.

[4] Alice Cary, "Nobility", contained in Roy J. Cook, ed., *One Hundred and One Famous Poems* (Chicago: Contemporary Books, Inc., 1958), pp. 111-12.

A Prerequisite of Enlightenment

> You are lucky, Callicles, in having been initiated in the Great Mysteries before the Little; I did not think it was permitted.
>
> Socrates, Plato's *Gorgias*

The greater mysteries before the lesser - Socrates' words to young Callicles come amidst heated exchange concerning personal integrity and its worth to the one who possesses it.[5] They call to mind a kindred lesson from a more recent work. Some years ago a German scholar named Eugen Herrigel, intrigued by accounts of Zen Buddhism, ventured to Japan to know its wisdom firsthand. This experience, and its broader life lessons, are recounted in his marvelous little 1953 classic *Zen in the Art of Archery*.

Where to begin? Opting, on recommendation, to practice through an applied art, Herrigel chooses the bow and arrow. It is relevantly similar, he imagines, to shooting a rifle, which he has done. But Zen archery, it turns out, is like nothing he has seen.

---

[5] See Plato's *Gorgias* 481b and following. (Hamilton and Cairns)

Day in and day out, Herrigel stands in front of the target drawing his bow. Grasping the bow, nocking the arrow, raising and loosing - each part of the exercise, he finds, is a mystery unto itself. Even breathing, the very first action in life, is relearned as an integral part of the process.

On the face of it, little is accomplished. The target is only ten feet away. But there is a reason. The object is not merely shooting practice, but something more. The master wishes to awaken something within his student, to bring out of his nature a truth that will stand him well in archery and in life. He, too, has an aim. He seeks to awaken in this student a new mode of being, to create an attunement of shooter with target that ordinary practice cannot comprehend.

To this end, lessons continue in small tasks of instrument and spirit. Loosing the arrow in the right manner is a conundrum that brings endless frustration. Weeks pass and Herrigel is still unable to release his shot in the manner sought. Time and again he is told to "let go," to allow something to happen independently of conscious effort. The exercise, he is told, is egoless. Real archery is not mere exercise, but a ceremony that exemplifies the Great Doctrine. The proper shot must fall as snow falls from the leaf without a stir.

Still trying without success, Herrigel one day happens on a way to release the shot. It looks like the right one - close enough, it seems, to convince. He offers this to the master, who watches and then asks for a repeat.

Seeing that the success is not genuine, the master announces the end of all instruction. A great deal of friendly intercession is needed before he can be persuaded to resume the lessons. He does so only on the condition that the Great Doctrine will not be violated in this manner again.

There is a valuable lesson in this story, for it tells us something about the first things, the things that begin any real effort at self-improvement. Nothing that is truly valuable can be gained by means of dissimulation. Often we look for ways to achievement that are shorter, less difficult, than the ones required. We try to gain by means of false impression. Herrigel's story reminds us that the lesser things come before the greater, that genuine development has its foundation in honesty. We must confront the task in a spirit of forthrightness and respect.

A Lesson from Benjamin Franklin

> As I knew, or thought I knew, what was right and wrong, I did not see why I might not always do the one and avoid the other. But I soon found I had undertaken a task of more difficulty than I had imagined.
>
> Benjamin Franklin, *The Art of Virtue*

Everyone, perhaps, has some notion of what distinguishes a high specimen of humanity from a middling or inferior one. But how many of us ever set out to keep track of ourselves in this regard?

While still in his twenties, Benjamin Franklin conceived the "bold and arduous project," as he would later call it, of achieving moral perfection. If the task seemed easy at first, he soon learned otherwise. While guarding against one fault, "I was often surprised by another; habit took the advantage of inattention; inclination was sometimes too strong for reason."

Mere conviction that virtue makes for a better life, he concluded, is not enough to insure improvement. Contrary habits must be actively broken and good ones acquired before we can manage *"a steady, uniform rectitude of conduct.*"[6]

Franklin devised a method. He began by setting out a table of virtues, distinguishing one from another where the commentary of other authors had blurred them together.[7] He proceeded to keep a daily record of success and failure with respect to each,

> *My intention being to acquire the habitude of all these virtues, I judged it would be well not to distract my attention by attempting the whole at once, but to fix it on one of them at a time; and, when I should be master of that, to proceed to another, and so on till I had gone through the thirteen* ...

Since some virtues might aid in the acquisition of others, Franklin gave them an order. Thus *temperance*, for example, which "tends to procure that coolness and clearness of head, which is so necessary where constant vigilance was to be kept up," preceded *silence* (i. e., the habit of withholding destructive or trifling speech), which would be of use in cultivating others in turn.

Not satisfied to keep merely a running estimate, Franklin lined out a book. He listed virtues in a side column

---

[6] This passage, from Franklin's *Autobiography*, is quoted by George L. Rogers in his annotated edition of Franklin's *The Art of Virtue* (Eden Prairie, Minnesota: Acorn Press, 1996), p. 41.

[7] These were, at last, thirteen: Temperance, Silence, Order, Resolution, Frugality, Industry, Sincerity, Justice, Moderation, Cleanliness, Tranquillity, Chastity, and Humility.

with the days of the week across the top. He then proceeded to devote one week to each of the virtues in succession. This enabled him to go through a complete "course" in thirteen weeks, and four such courses in a year.

It was an education. Franklin was surprised to find himself more full of faults than he would have imagined. Yet this painstaking exercise allowed him the satisfaction of seeing bad traits diminish with time and attention. On the whole, he writes,

> *though I never arrived at the perfection I had been so ambitious of obtaining, but fell far short of it, yet I was, by the endeavor, a better and happier man than I otherwise should have been if I had not attempted it ...*[8]

---

[8] *Ibid.*, p. 48.

Inward Vision

> He learned to close his eyes and hit. Not during the game - the night before, visualizing where the pitch might come and at what speed.
>
> Rick Reilly,
> describing St. Louis slugger Mark McGwire [9]

The mind is a well-spring. All manner of writers have remarked on its capacity, upon powers and resources deepwithin us that we may seldom stop to consider. Their observations span a wide range of circumstance.

To change your life, writes Norman Vincent Peale, begin to think in a new way. Start to form a picture of things the way they should be. "Hold that picture," he says, "develop it firmly in all details, believe in it, pray about it, work at it, and you can actualize it according to that mental image."[10]

"Whatever your situation may be," he insists,

---

[9] See Reilly's "The Good Father", *Sports Illustrated* (New York: Time Inc., 1998), issue of Sept. 7th. This article, written late in McGwire's monumental 1998 season, describes his return to baseball superstardom after several years of uncertainty and professional failure.

[10] *The Power of Positive Thinking*, p. 170.

> you can improve it. First, quiet your mind so that inspirations may rise from its depths. Believe that God is now helping you. Visualize achievement. Organize your life on a spiritual basis so that God's principles work within you. Hold firmly in your mind a picture not of failure but of success. Do these things and creative thoughts will flow freely from your mind.[11]

This, adds Peale, is one of the greatest laws in all of life.

> Fervently do I wish that I had discovered it as a very young man. It dawned upon me much later in life and I have found it to be one of the greatest if not my greatest discovery, outside of my relationship to God. And in a deep sense this law is a factor in one's relationship with God because it channels God's power into personality.[12]

This same law is cited in places far from the pulpit. Athletes, as the opening quotation suggests, work often at gaining mental focus, at *seeing* their success before the fact. People working to improve their physical appearance and condition are advised to hold in their minds an image of how they wish to look. The firmer this picture, the more certain the result. It is as if the mind, at some deep level, works to bring about the state of affairs that it suggests.

---

[11] *Ibid.*, p. 176.

[12] *Ibid.*, p. 170.

One also finds this principle in philosophical traditions far removed from Peale's own Protestant Christianity. The book *You - Forever* by popular occult writer Lobsang Rampa offers testimony.

Our time on earth is limited, writes Rampa, and soon we will leave this present life behind. Thus if we are wise, we will make our real investment not in this world, but in our own development. For this reason Rampa does not advocate material gain as an end unto itself. Yet we have within us, he explains, untapped abilities that we may put to use however we choose. There are laws built into the fabric of the universe, laws that make it possible for us to get (for better or worse) anything that we want. The mind can give us all that we ask if we use it.

You must decide, says Rampa, what you want - precisely and in definite terms, and you must say it. "It will not do," he explains, "to say you want a lot of money, it will not do to say that you want a new car or a new wife or a new husband." You must instead be exact. "You must visualize it - picture it in your mind - and hold that picture firmly before you."[13]

---

[13] Lobsang Rampa, *You - Forever* (London: Corgi Books, 1965), p. 171.

The Verge of Greatness

> "Dad, listen. I tried as hard as I could. And what for? Where am I headed? I'm telling you it's no use and that's all there is to it. I'm not -"
>
> "Now you shut up! I don't want to hear that whining! I thought I raised a man, not a coward!" It was as though he had leveled a double-barreled shotgun at my head.
>
> "Dad, please ..."
>
> "Sure, I'll please you. I'm gonna pack your stuff, that's what I'm gonna do. You can go back and work in the mines like me!"
>
> The sight of him, his face as white as a sheet, his eyes full of sorrow and shame as he flung shirts and socks into my bag, all the time muttering, "I thought I raised a man."
>
> Mickey Mantle, *The Mick*

I was born in March of 1951. That spring a 19-year old phenomenon from Spanivaw, Oklahoma, was cracking the lineup of the fabled New York Yankees. Veteran observers said that he had more God-given talent than any player they had seen. A few years later I found baseball, the Yankees, and Mantle by neighborhood contagion.

Saturday mornings were a showcase of Yankee glory. Immortal St. Louis righthander Dizzy Dean and Dodger shortstop Pee Wee Reese called the play-by-play. Like their contemporary Don Dunphy, who announced Friday night fight action from ringside, these men did not just report the event. They thrilled to it. It was an era when men with microphones had respect for the men who plied the trade. There were no snide remarks, no tortured puns or computer-statistic landslides. If there came a lull, Diz wasn't worried. He'd look around and show you some kid who wanted his dad to buy him a baseball. Or maybe he would break into a verse of "Wabash Cannonball."

If there is one image that remains in my mind from those years (they were indeed, as later culture would call them, *happy days*), it is the black-and-white vision of Mantle's swing and the camera panning up into the right-field cavern of Yankee Stadium. "Swung on ... *and there she goes!*" The ball landed in the third tier. Diz knew it was gone when it left the bat.

Mutt Mantle was a miner who wanted his boy to be a champion. To this end the son Mickey Charles was raised. Once old enough to swing a bat, he faced the backyard fire of his father and his uncle, who soon were challenging him with fastballs and curves that made him a hitter.

He also learned, at Mutt's insistence, to hit from each side of the plate, opposite the hand of the pitcher. In this way, a curve from either side would break in and not away. It was easier to follow.

Years later, Mantle would remember how he was returned to the Kansas farm club that first summer for "seasoning." Touted only weeks earlier as the game's next superstar, he now found himself struggling against minor-league throwers and verging upon disaster. At last he summoned his father to his hotel room and said that he wanted to quit. Expecting sympathy, he got the lambasting of his life. He had no business in baseball, said Mutt, if he could not fight his way back into it.

There is something to learn from the story of every great success - athlete, actor, writer, politician. Superstars, we imagine, are a breed apart. Yet dig into each story and you find the same thing. Trial. Struggle. Outright humiliation. The heavyweight champion once got a whipping from his older sister. The Oscar-winner left the stage in mid-act. The great sculptor could not buy his way into the school of fine arts. Always, it seems, is a test, earthy and plain, before stellar achievement.

Baseball, like other sports, is a game of inches and fine fractions of inches where the least difference in mind set can mean everything. Mantle returned to the Yankees late that summer. He never saw the minor leagues again. In years to come he would wreak havoc on American League pitching, launching home runs out of stadiums and becoming the league's Most Valuable Player three times. In 1956 and 1957, he had two of the greatest individual seasons in baseball history. Despite recurring leg injuries, he was acknowledged as being, for several years, the fastest runner, home plate to first, in the game. It has been written that no man ever swung harder at a pitched ball.

We are reminded, in Mantle's go-round with his father in Kansas, how little separates failure from championship. Even the most talented among us must give all that we have for what we want. If not, others will. There is an old adage in boxing: A good fighter in great shape beats a great fighter in good shape. Sheer force of will may carry the day.

From that scene we learn, too, that we are not always helping others by sharing in their misery. Left to themselves they may never know what they are meant to achieve. Had Mutt Mantle been easier on his son, we might never have seen the Mick. More than anything, we must bear in mind how our own frame of mind can defeat us, how a brief bout of depression may conceal immanent victory.

Soul-Making and Its Direction

> The good that outshines all ill is not a paradise long since lost but a kingdom which is yet to come in its full glory and permanence.
>
> John Hick, *Evil and the God of Love*

From the drama of the playing field to the arena of life: An old problem has vexed philosophers like no other. It is the problem of evil - simply put, it is the problem of how we can believe in a God of love when the world contains so much pain.

Not all persons are troubled by it. Good and evil, some say, are "relative." Or they cannot exist, we hear, without each other. But the problem becomes more difficult on reflection. A horrifying conversation is related in Dostoevsky's great novel *The Brothers Karamazov*.[14] In it Ivan Karamazov challenges his devout young brother Alyosha to explain how the world can contain certain atrocities. Ivan describes instances of the torture and murder of children, events beyond rational explanation.

---

[14] See Fyodor Dostoevsky, *The Brothers Karamazov*. Trans. Constance Garnett (New York: The Modern Library, 1950). This discussion takes place in Book II, Part 4, in a section entitled "Rebellion".

Trite answers, abstract solutions, we learn in this passage, do not avail. If there is an answer, it must speak to the pain of the very souls who trod the earth and in time are lain beneath it. In order to understand evil, says John Hick, we must understand the role that it plays in our own destiny.[15]

A *theodicy*[16] may look to the past for its explanation, say, to some original "fall" that has condemned us to hardship. Yet the better, more constructive explanation, believes Hick, looks to the future. The world is an arena of soul-making. It calls forth responses that a softer world might not.

Here we are given not punishment, but opportunity. Here, as free agents, in a world without guarantee, we have the chance to become citizens of eternity. There will come a day when we see these brief lives as but stages on the way to an end that infinitely outweighs our trials, and so may justify all that has happened on the way to its realization.

---

[15] See Hick's classic discussion of the problem of evil in *Evil and the God of Love* (New York: Harper and Row, 1966). See also his discussion of Ivan and Alyosha in his *Death and Eternal Life* (Louisville: Westminster / John Knox Press, 1994).

[16] This term comes from the Greek words *theos* (god) and *dike* (justice) and refers to an effort to reconcile God's love with the existence of suffering.

... thy actions betray thee to be a coward;
therefore stand up and fight.

III

Heroism

What is a hero? The ancients used the term to describe such figures as Hector and Aeneas, warriors and sojourners whose deeds stirred their souls. These individuals were fancied, at times, as gods, or as half-offspring mortal and divine. But they were never quite divorced from their humanity.[1]

Today we use the term widely, bestowing it upon athletes, authors, and champions of social justice. We speak of heroes in medicine and the theoretical sciences. Yet the word retains something of its original flavor, reflecting in each case our special admiration of what is extraordinary and still human. In the hero is a will to transcend limit, and so potentially in ourselves.

---

[1] In such individuals, it seems, extraordinary power meets with vulnerability. In them, explains Carl Kerenyi, "The glory of the divine ... is strangely combined with the shadow of mortality." See Kerenyi's work *The Heroes of the Greeks* (New York: Grove Press, Inc., 1960), p. 3.

The Founding of a Nation

> *These are the times that try men's souls. The Summer soldier and the sunshine patriot will, in this crisis, shrink from the service of their country; but he that stands it now, deserves the love and thanks of man and woman.*
>
> Thomas Paine, *The American Crisis*

Things could not have looked worse. It was December of 1776 and the Revolution was in collapse. General George Washington had suffered massive defeats, and there was no prospect, it seemed, of anything more to come. His makeshift army of farmers, storekeepers, and frontiersmen seemed no match for thousands of British regulars and their paid Hessian allies.

It all looked quite hopeless, when on Christmas night Washington made an outrageous decision. Rather than retreat, rather than surrender, he did the last thing that anyone, on either side might have expected. He chose to push the attack. That evening he and his men, all but beaten, climbed into their boats and took the offensive. They made their way in blackness across the freezing Delaware River, great hunks of ice hammering without pity the whole way.

Reaching shore at three in the morning, the troops marched forward in murderous cold. The roads, notes historian Robert Leckie,[2] were an ordeal of ice and blood. In the morning, Washington's major James Wilkinson could follow the troops ahead by the trail of red snow.

The American rebels had cannon, but would they be in condition to fire? Gunners commanded by Captain Alexander Hamilton struck their torches. "The cannon roared and bucked. American cheers mingled with the shrieks of Hessian soldiers stricken by grapeshot. Soldiers came forward into the mouths of enemy cannon." Firearms soaked, patriots fixed the bayonet. Some were able to retreat into houses to repair their weapons. Others went forward.

It was a rout. The victory at Trenton resurrected American spirit. Washington moved on to Princeton where he won again. From this day forward, the English knew that they were in a fight. The hardship would continue. Washington and his men would spend an agonizing winter at Valley Forge, Pennsylvania, lest the functioning capitol of Philadelphia fall into enemy hands. No group of men ever braved harder conditions. But in the end was a victory that would capture the imagination of the world.

---

[2] For a thorough account of the Revolution, grim and unsparing in its details, see Robert Leckie, *George Washington's War - the Saga of the American Revolution* (New York: HarperCollins, 1992).

Opportunity

> Fight, and you may die. Run, and you will live ... at least awhile. And dying in your beds, many years from now, would you be willing to trade all the days, from this day to that, for one chance - just one chance - to come back here and tell our enemies that they may take our lives ... but they'll never take our *freedom*!
>
> William Wallace,
> *Braveheart* (the motion picture)

We have seen how one act of sheer audacity may steer the course of history. The words just cited are attributed to William Wallace in the film *Braveheart*, a semi-historical epic that tells another story of liberation, in this case the Scottish break from oppressive English rule in the fourteenth century. They describe the situation of a courageous handful of medieval revolutionaries, outnumbered and overmatched, on the field of battle. They describe, as well, our own daily challenge.

There are times when we are faced with choice between principle and advantage. There are many occasions for this choice. It may involve, for example, the chance to gain profit by means of deceit, or unfair advantage. Or it may mean the chance to gain popularity by compromising our beliefs. At times we are faced with the question of whether or not we should speak out against prevailing social and political trend.

Integrity, in such cases, may put us at odds with opinion, with the power structure, with whatever is the received wisdom of the day. Insight and popularity, in fact, are inherently in tension with each other. The beliefs of the masses, of professional and educational institutions, of most of our peers, reflect in many cases not intelligence, but the broad forces of social trend.

In these times we are tested. Principle may cost us promotion, acceptance, friendship, positive image in the eyes of others. One day it may cost our lives. When faced with difficult choices we might ask ourselves the question that Wallace asks his own forces. If we ignore principle for security, what will we think about this choice, years later, in our final hour?

Spirituality and the Battlefield

Thou talkest like a wise man, but thy actions betray thee to be a coward; therefore stand up and fight.

Sri Krishna, the *Bhagavad-Gita*

The Bhagavad-Gita, or Song of the Lord, was composed, as part of a much longer epic, some time during the last few centuries before the common era. There is perhaps no more popular or influential piece of literature in the religious heritage of India. In it a young *kshatriya* (a member of the classical warrior caste) named Arjuna is called upon to wage war against a neighboring army.[3]

The opening books of this story describe Arjuna's dilemma as he looks out on an impending carnage. Seeing this, he asks his charioteer Krishna[4] if there is any point to the undertaking. He has no wish to kill or to be killed. Can it be his duty to do violence to these other men?

---

[3] For an account of classical Indian warfare, see A. L. Basham, *The Wonder that was India* (New York: Grove Press, 1954), pp. 122-36. The caste rank included *brahmin* (priest), *kshatriya* (warrior), *vaisya* (merchant), and *shudra* (laborer).

[4] Krishna, as it turns out, is an incarnation of God. See related discussion in chapters 8 and 10 of this volume.

Krishna answers that it is Arjuna's place - his sacred obligation - to fight the battle. Should Arjuna refuse this task, should he find it too brutal or repugnant, he gives way to the lesser part of himself. Krishna chides him for losing heart and bids him to rise to the occasion.

It is a strange thing to find, says commentator Swami Prabhavananda, in literature of the spirit. One does not expect glorification of combat here, of all places. How can we square this message with the claim that the *Gita* is concerned with religious development?

There are ways to explain this situation without supposing that the *Gita* condones warfare. One may view the setting, for example, not as a real battlefield, but as a symbolic confrontation of good and evil. Yet while this reading is possible, says Prabhavananda, it is not necessary. For physical struggle, and even mortal combat, has its place in the spiritual drama.

It is an assumption of classical Indian philosophy that human beings differ profoundly in their capacities and inclinations. They differ likewise in their levels of spiritual development. Thus they come to this world fitted to different tasks: Some may need to prove themselves on the field of honor. Others may not. But for those in the appropriate condition, physical danger serves a purpose. It provides an opportunity for ultimate risk and sacrifice.

This variety of roles and tasks does not imply variety in principle. While our duties vary, they are united in a singularity of purpose. There is but one enlightenment, and each particular life-duty reflects the need of an individual in relation to the goal. The non-resistance demanded of a *brahmin* priest, for example, is appropriate to his own spiritual condition. Practiced by another, it might proceed from weakness. To insist upon the same duty for everyone, says Prabhavananda, would require more of some persons than they can presently manage.

It is wrong, he continues, to insist that individuals are "created equal," if this means that they have now the same aptitude and are fitted to the same life-enterprise. Nothing could be further from the facts of experience. We need to admit that there are different kinds of people in the world and that they vary in their basic talents and dispositions. We must also realize that our progress in this life is made relative to our own present conditions and inward resources.

Moral Confrontation

> It is ... by an act of courage that we begin to *exist* ethically.
>
> William Barrett, *Irrational Man*

Courage, as many writers have observed, involves more than the battlefield. Quiet choices, made alone and in darkness, provide equally good examples. The worth of an action is not measured by public drama. Within each of us is a field of combat entirely real.

The philosopher Soren Kierkegaard wrote his works around the middle of the nineteenth century. All around, he observed, people were engaged in the effort to make life easier and more convenient. Perhaps life, in some ways, was too easy. Perhaps, he imagined, there was a place for someone who would make it more difficult.

Some things, thought Kierkegaard, were inherently difficult. Or they would be, at least, if we understood what they involved. He was disgusted with attitudes toward such things as truth and salvation that prevailed in his day. He was amazed, in particular, at the tendency of most individuals to think of themselves as *Christian* without ever having made a decisive individual choice in the matter.

He laughed, too, at the tendency of certain types to seek out defenses of their faith in order to salvage their intellectual dignity.[5] For surely, he thought, faith requires before everything else the rejection of such worldly concern. If we trust in the reality of another world, we will not seek out popular approval in this one.

Kierkegaard reacted also against the whole tradition of philosophy that purported to have intellectual grasp of the human condition. The condition of a human being, he insisted, was a spiritual event. Its progress came in stages, not by mere insight but through concrete choices.

The first of these is the so-called aesthetic[6] stage, the stage at which the primary concern is self-entertainment. The second is the ethical. It transcends this first level, for it provides a whole new basis for action.

---

[5] Suppose, says Kierkegaard, that a man wishes to have faith, but also desires intellectual confidence in what he believes. Now, he writes, "the comedy begins. The object of his faith becomes almost probable, as good as probable, extremely and emphatically probable. He has completed his investigations, and he ventures to claim for himself that he does not believe as shoemakers and tailors and other simple folk believe, but that he has also understood himself in his believing. Strange understanding!" See Soren Kierkegaard, *Concluding Unscientific Postscript*. Trans. David F. Swenson and Walter Lowrie (Princeton: Princeton University Press, 1944), p. 189.

[6] See William Barrett, *Irrational Man* (New York: Doubleday, 1990). As Barrett observes, the word 'aesthetic' has its roots in the Greek *theatai*, a verb meaning to behold. Persons in a *theater* stand in a passive relation to what is on the stage; they do not fully enter into it. *Theoretical* activity is likewise cognitive, detached, and removed from total involvement. (See related discussion in chapter 7.)

Kierkegaard, writes William Barrett, has an understanding in advance of much recent psychology. Over the past hundred years we have tried to move beyond old ideas of good and evil by means of clinical diagnosis. But these things, as Kierkegaard realizes, cannot be analyzed away. We gain nothing by trying to understand, say, malice or gross deceit in terms of *neurosis*.[7]

Nor is scholarship a guarantee of moral worth. It is one thing, says Barrett, to make a formal career of ethics. It is quite another to face a moral demand.[8] A philosopher's life may abound in notions of value without feeling "the bite of the ethical upon it." Our real choice is not one between ideas, but one by which "we summon good and bad into existence for ourselves."[9]

---

[7] The closer we get to the so-called neurotic, he explains, "the more we are assailed by the sheer human perverseness, the wilfulness, of his attitude." (p. 170)

[8] Or in C. S. Lewis' trenchant words, "In battle it is not syllogisms that will keep the reluctant nerves and muscles to their post in the third hour of the bombardment." (See *The Abolition of Man*, p. 35.)

[9] *Irrational Man*, p. 165.

IV

Truth and Rationality

Before all things, decrees Heraclitus, is the *logos*, the primal truth that bestows order upon the world.[1] Reason, *logic*, is vital to civilization and to individual human progress. This chapter explores its defining nature.

With reason comes *objectivity* - the transcendence, in other words, of our own peculiar limit. From this new vantage point we gain insight; we gain also some measure of freedom, of independence from prevailing societal trend. Reaching this higher ground is more than an intellectual exercise; it requires strength, self-sufficiency, the frame of mind and soul that prizes truth above comfort or fashion. In meeting this challenge we rise above circumstance and enter upon intellectual adulthood.

---

[1] For text and commentary, see G. S. Kirk and J. E. Raven, eds., *The Presocratic Philosophers* (Cambridge: Cambridge University Press, 1969), pp. 182 and following.

At the Water's Edge

> I do not know what I may appear to the world; but to myself I seem to have been only like a boy, playing on the sea-shore, and diverting myself, in now and then finding a smoother pebble or prettier shell than ordinary, whilst the great ocean of truth lay all undiscovered before me.
>
> Isaac Newton, personal conversation

Science, say some, is the crowning attainment of mankind; by its light, by its hard and wholesome integrity, human enterprise is lifted above the darkness of ignorance and superstition.

Yet it is characteristic of the greatest scientists that they are more than mere intellects or masters of fact. They are capable of genuine, even childlike, wonder. Newton's comment,[2] made late in life, reveals an element of true genius, a capacity to see things from above and outside one's own historical position. In it is the voice of a man who not only sees the world, but marvels at it, one who perceives in it both fact and splendor.

---

[2] This statement, reprinted often, is noted by Gale E. Christianson on page 574 of his book *In the Presence of the Creator - Isaac Newton and His Times* (New York: The Free Press, 1984).

Newton, of course, no longer has final word in the sciences. Yet in his statement we find something that is timeless, a genuine intelligence conjoined with modesty. In it we find inspiration. The image of a child at water's edge reminds us that the voyage is scarcely begun. Yet this same image is cause for intellectual thrill. Each step on the way is an advancement upon our previous condition. Aristotle[3] says quite famously that human beings by nature desire to know. As we persevere we find that it is indeed in learning - in seeking, creating, and discovering - that we are most alive. Each grain of effort makes us more than we were before, makes us indeed more ourselves.

The ocean is vast; as such it represents the reality, the miracle, by which we are confronted, in which we are submerged, each day of our lives. It provides an image both daunting and fabulous. The universe is truth, but more than this, it is an outrageous gift. Such is the prospect that life holds out to us; to know more, to plunge into this infinity and in so doing to rejoice in it.

---

[3] Book *Alpha* of Aristotle's *Metaphysics* begins with the observation that "All men naturally have an impulse to get knowledge." See Richard Hope, translator, *Aristotle - Metaphysics* (Ann Arbor, Michigan: The University of Michigan Press, 1994).

The Ideal of Rationality

> The lifting of reason fully out of the primeval waters of the unconscious is a Greek achievement.
>
> William Barrett, *Irrational Man*

It is the Greeks, writes William Barrett, who give us reason.[4] The Greeks, of course, were not the first people to think about things. But they were the first to make reason a science, to define its principles and make it an object unto itself. By this leap western civilization gains its distinctive character.

Prior to this, its culture is young. Its first principles, notes W. T. Jones, are glorified human personalities. They are much like children "who happen, through some paradox of nature, to be endowed with great power."[5]

Their own origin is a strange abyss. First, writes Hesiod,

---

[4] William Barrett, *Irrational Man* (New York: Doubleday, 1958). See especially chapter 4, "Hebraism and Hellenism".

[5] W. T. Jones, *A History of Western Philosophy* (Fort Worth, Texas: Harcourt Brace Jovanovich College Publishers, 1980), volume I, p. 5.

> came the Chasm; and then broad-breasted Earth, secure seat for ever of all the immortals who occupy the peak of snowy Olympus; the misty Tartara in a remote recess of the broad-breasted Earth; and Eros, the most handsome among the immortal gods, dissolver of flesh, who overcomes reason and purpose in the breasts of all gods and all men.[6]

Out of the sea is born Aphrodite from the severed flesh of Great Heaven, castrated by his son Kronus. The Rivers are sons of Oceanus. Thea, lying with Hyperion, gives birth "to the mighty Sun and shining Moon, and to Dawn, who makes light for all who dwell on earth and for the immortal gods who live in the wise heaven."

Such stories may intrigue, may captivate, yet they do not provide rational explanation.[7] They do not yield elements or principles that account in consistent fashion for the things that we see around us. It all changes in the sixth century B. C. in the town of Miletus on the seaboard of Asia Minor, where a handful of pioneers seek to explain the world with idea.

---

[6] See Hesiod, *Theogony*; bound in one volume with *Works and Days*. Trans. M. L. West (Oxford: Oxford University Press, 1988), p. 6.

[7] Thus there is no final and consistent explanation, in these stories, of what occurs in the world. The gods, at times, seem to have ultimate power; yet above them, it sometimes appears, is a blind and inscrutable *fate* to which even Zeus must yield. See *A History of Western Philosophy*, vol. I, pp. 4-8.

Thales,[8] for one, names water as the cause of all things.[9] His effort invites others: Reality is *apeiron*,[10] the undistinguished, from which come basic opposites (hot and cold, wet and dry, and the like). Or it is *aer*,[11] a single stuff that becomes many by its density and rarefaction.

Such views may seem primitive. But with them dawns the awareness that reality is intelligible, that it conforms to reason and so is accessible to the mind. From this time forward, writes Jones, "there are indeed *theories* - public assertions, not private fantasies."

Here, then, is the beginning of objectivity. Here, too, the well-spring of science - knowledge, as John Locke would later say, of things "as they are in themselves."[12] The capacity for such thought, the notion of a truth distinct from appearance, is our Greek inheritance.

---

[8] Or something like water - the Greek *hudros* connoting liquid.

[9] Thales' rationale has been discussed many times. Very likely he was impressed with the plasticity of the substance - its capacity to become, under varying conditions, solid, liquid, or gas. Water inheres in many things, and it seems to be powerfully involved in the origin and maintenance of life.

[10] Literally, "the unbounded" - the view of Anaximander.

[11] Often translated as 'air' or 'mist', Anaximenes' key word is interesting for its suggestion that differences of *quality* in the world are explainable, at bottom, in terms of *quantity*.

[12] John Locke, *An Essay Concerning Human Understanding* (London: J. M. Dent and Sons Ltd., 1947). See Book IV, "Of Knowledge, Certain and Probable".

Respect for Truth

> He who knows only his own side of the case, knows little of that.
>
> John Stuart Mill, "On Liberty"

What does it mean to know something? What does it mean to value the truth, to seek and obtain it? When are we justified in holding a given belief?

We imagine, for practical purposes, that our beliefs are reliable, that we know some things, moreover, with certainty. Yet few of us, by the same token, stop to ask what gives us this logical right - to ask what may distinguish, for example, a sound belief from an unsound one, or knowledge from accidental truth. The issue of belief and its justification is discussed by the English philosopher John Stuart Mill in his essay "On Liberty".[13]

The theme of this discourse, as its title suggests, is that of personal freedom. To what extent should individuals in a civilized state be allowed to do as they please?

---

[13] The relevant portion of this essay is reprinted in Peyton E. Richter and Walter L. Fogg, eds., *Philosophy Looks to the Future* (Prospect Heights, Illinois: Waveland Press, 1978).

The society that prizes truth, thinks Mill, will grant its citizens whole and unqualified freedom of expression. If all mankind but one, he says famously, were of one opinion, that majority would be no more justified in silencing this lone exception than he would be in silencing them.

The saying has become popular, and like many such sayings, it is cited with abandon. Some take it as an indication that every viewpoint is equally legitimate, or that every one is entitled to the same respect. Yet this, as the essay itself reveals, is the last thing that Mill intends to say. The real advantage in hearing different viewpoints is that we may discern their worth.[14]

The society that fosters respect for truth, thinks Mill, will fare better than one that does not. For this reason no opinion should be banned from the public forum. Nor is an opinion confirmed simply because it now enjoys popular - or even educated - acceptance. An unpopular view is no less worth protecting. Whether this view is true or false, we will be better for hearing it. We will lose something by its omission.

---

[14] Another popular notion is that Mill is citing an abstract individual *right* that holds in principle against the state. While this conception of a right figures in much of modern philosophy, Mill himself does not rely upon it. The basis of his argument, as he states, is *utility* - the net sum and quality of happiness enjoyed by those in the society.

This is surely the case when the banned opinion turns out to be true. But if we think about it, says Mill, this is no less the case when the opinion turns out to be false. For in actively weighing this view, in passing responsible judgment upon it, we strengthen our understanding. Nor should any view, however likely its truth, be immune from question. No matter how obvious this view may seem, "if it is not fully, frequently, and fearlessly discussed, it will be held as a dead dogma, not a living truth." A belief, even if it is true, ought not to win by default - "this is not the way," says Mill, "in which truth ought to be held by a rational being." Such truth is not knowledge, but "one superstition the more, accidentally clinging to the words which enunciate a truth."

If we value the truth, we will not adopt views simply because they are convenient. We will not favor them, say, because we have been raised with them, or because they win us approval. Rationality requires more. We have it on record, observes Mill, that the Roman orator Cicero always studied his adversary's case with at least as great intensity as his own. It is a difficult method, but one that deserves to be imitated "by all who study any subject in order to arrive at the truth."[15]

---

[15] *Ibid.*, p. 319.

An individual may prevail in argument, may persuade others of his opinion against argument to the contrary. But this is not the same as knowing the truth of that opinion. For however good his reasons, if he has not confronted the opposing view in its best possible light, such an individual cannot claim to be fully justified in rejecting it. He must know the other side in its most plausible form, must "feel the whole force of the difficulty," before deciding.

Ninety-nine percent of so-called educated men, says Mill, are in this position. They may have keenness and academic reputation on their side. Yet "they have never thrown themselves into the mental position" of those who think differently from themselves.

Respect for the truth is thus a rare thing indeed. Our civil liberty is justified, thinks Mill, by the fact that a society permitting freedom of thought (and thus also the kindred freedoms of speech and writing) permits a more active search for truth than does one steered by private interest or political vogue. A society that carries out this search, thinks Mill, will enjoy greater well-being over time.

Transcending Present Conditions

> ... our own age is also "a period," and certainly has, like all periods, its own characteristic illusions.
>
> C. S. Lewis, *Surprised by Joy*

Truth is more than prevailing opinion. The worth of an idea is not measured by its acceptability in popular circles. If we are to think seriously about anything, we must first establish our mental independence from those feelings and assumptions that now hold sway.

Real insight is gained not by allegiance to the going opinion, but by the active and independent exercise of our own critical faculties. "Be suspicious of convention," writes Epictetus in his manual *The Art of Living*.[16] "Take charge of your own thinking. Rouse yourself from the daze of unexamined habit."[17]

---

[16] Epictetus, *The Art of Living* (San Francisco: HarperCollins, 1995), p. 92. Edited and translated by Sharon Lebell.

[17] The world, he observes, is full of misleading assumptions. One is tempted to say, for example, "I am richer than you; therefore, I am better than you." From the fact that one is richer, it only follows that one has a greater supply of material possessions. Anything else is a separate question. Quality of life is dependent on character, which is "independent of property or persuasive speech." (See, for example, p. 72, "Clear Thinking is Vital".)

We must become self-reliant. "To believe your own thought," writes Emerson, "that is genius." The great man, he explains, "is he who in the midst of the crowd keeps with perfect sweetness the independence of solitude."[18]

Novelist and philosopher C. S. Lewis relates an episode in his own development.[19] He describes his encounter at Oxford with a man named Owen Barfield, who became (notwithstanding their immense personal differences) Lewis' lifelong friend. Go-rounds with Barfield, says Lewis, destroyed in him his tendency toward "chronological snobbery" - his uncritical acceptance of the prevailing outlook, and his thought that "whatever has gone out of date is on that account discredited."[20] The present age has, like any other, its characteristic illusions. Such illusions may lurk in assumptions "so ingrained in the age that no one dares to attack or feels it necessary to defend them."[21]

---

[18] See Emerson's "Self-Reliance", contained in Robert D. Richardson, Jr., ed., *Emerson: Selected Essays, Lectures, and Poems* (New York: Bantam Books, 1990).

[19] C. S. Lewis, *Surprised by Joy* (San Diego: Harcourt and Company, 1955).

[20] *Ibid.*, p. 207.

[21] *Ibid.*, p. 208.

V

Moral Value

Life, as we have seen, concerns more than just material fact. It has to do also with value - with ideals, principles, standards by which we measure our own worth. How should I behave? What sort of man or woman should I strive to become? These questions arise in every life, and the way that we live depends upon how we answer them.

But what is value? Ideas abound concerning its nature. It is, say some, an accident of our chemistry, or a by-product of the culture in which we are raised. Others believe that value is something more, that it is specially authoritative and perhaps even supernatural. In this section we will examine ideas concerning moral value and its meaning.

Out of the Cave

> What, then, Glaucon, would be the study that would draw the soul away from the world of becoming to the world of being?
>
> Socrates, Plato's *Republic*

It is a haunting story, one that has held the imagination for more than two thousand years. In Book VII of *The Republic*, Plato speaks of captives who sit chained in a cave below ground where they have spent their lives watching shadows on the wall. Lacking a point of comparison, they take these images for reality.[1]

One day a captive is freed and turned around to the truth. It is a new experience, unlike any he has had. Yet in time, and with assistance, he makes his way upward into the light of day. What awaits is an astonishment - stars, the moon, and last the sun - all wondrously different from what lay below.

It is a picture, says Plato, of the human condition. We are like unto this prisoner, who until now has seen only images. Our own world is the shadow, the inferior. Beyond it lies one greater.

---

[1] See *Republic* 514a and following. (Hamilton and Cairns)

This, too, is the voyage of philosophy - the turning, as it were, from the things of this world to the things of eternity. Its ascent is steep and rugged; its reward is at first uncertain. But in time, with effort and adjustment, we see its reality, surpassing this life as the light of the heavens surpasses that of the cave.

This higher world, thinks Plato, is the object of all real knowledge, of *wisdom, courage, justice* - qualities absolute and unchanging. Here we see truth only in its reflection. Yet this contact jars us, calls us back to something that precedes all mortal experience. It strikes a chord within our souls, informs us of a truth that is beyond appearance. In reason, in wisdom, in noble action is expressed timeless reality.

All real inquiry is an investigation of this higher world, the ground of truth and the residence of the soul. It is the world from which we have come and to which we return. Our departure from life here, insists Plato, is not death, but birth and homecoming. The story endures, some say, because it is "uplifting" or "picturesque." But if it is uplifting, if its picture is apt, then it must *raise* our apprehension. It must make us more than we were before reading it. Perhaps the secret of this story is its truth - the reality of a world that makes this one as dim, by comparison, as the outside world makes the dungeon.

Duty and Inclination

> *Duty is the necessity of acting from respect for the law.* I may have *inclination* for an object as the effect of my proposed action, but I cannot have *respect* for it, just for this reason, that it is an effect and not an energy of will.
>
> Immanuel Kant,
> *Metaphysical Foundations of Morals*

He is no easy read, this grim-sounding little Prussian who never went 40 miles beyond his native Koenigsberg. But when we look closely, we find something extraordinary. If Kant's life lacked breadth, it made up in depth, for his philosophy, like that of Plato, beckons us into the infinite.

Kant, to be sure, is a long way from Athens. He is born into a Pietist Lutheran family two centuries after the Reformation and during the rise of modern science. His understanding of value is accordingly different from that of his Greek predecessor. Where ethics, for Plato, concerns rational vision, for Kant it means sacred command. Yet he and Plato share something. In each of these men burns a vision of eternity and a profound respect for what is disclosed to us in moral experience.

Ethics, think some, is a cold and somber enterprise. Rules, regulations, things that proper individuals don't do - such talk seems tired today and too much given to self-restriction. In reading Kant we gain another insight. Value, we find, is no trifling matter. It is more than false pose or raised eyebrows. It is spiritual reality, profound and thrilling, that invests our lives with a meaning that is unconditional.[2]

Life, says Kant, contains many directives, many prescriptions for how we should behave. These "imperatives," as he calls them, are sometimes conditional. They are dependent, in other words, upon the want or circumstance of the moment. Thus I should buy my ticket today, for example, if I wish to be in Chicago next week. I had better work my deltoid muscles, provided that I am going to compete in bodybuilding. Such prescriptions are not absolute; they derive their worth from my own plans.

There is another imperative, says Kant, that is "categorical." It applies across all cases. This imperative provides an objective basis for my behavior. It overrides my preference, indeed it is sovereign in the scheme of practical decision-making. It is the law to which my actions, in principle, ought to conform.

---

[2] The *Metaphysical Foundations* is contained in its entirety in Carl J. Friedrich, ed., *The Philosophy of Kant* (New York: The Modern Library, 1993).

How does one know what this imperative requires? We discover its formula, thinks Kant, by the use of reason. Consider the following example. Suppose that I want a certain sum of money. I see, too, that I can obtain it by making a false promise to repay. This promise, then, is profitable. Is it morally sound?

What I must now ask myself, says Kant, is whether or not *I would be willing to live in a world* that follows my example. Suppose (to modify his own discussion just a little) that by pushing a button I could turn the whole world into people who behave always just as I intend to behave now. Would I do it? In that world, lying is standard behavior. Everyone makes promises like mine when they want something. But of course I cannot want to live in such a world.[3] For in it, promises express only desires. Hence my lie gets me nowhere.

Thus lying cannot be *universalized* as a form of human behavior. I must depend upon the honesty of others if my lie is to have effect. Thus in lying I will one thing for myself and another for others.

---

[3] See, for example, pp. 164-65 of the Friedrich edition. This test, believes Kant, applies not only to particular kinds of behavior, but to broad choices of lifestyle. Suppose, for example, that I have certain talents, but refuse to develop them because I prefer to live with minimal effort. Perhaps, in this case, the world *could* operate in such a fashion, but surely I cannot want it, for my own enjoyment would be diminished as a result.

This inconsistency, says Kant, tells me that lying is immoral. Hence the categorical imperative may be expressed by the command to act so that the maxim, or general rule, of our behavior is one that we want for mankind.

Deceit, Kant explains, is likewise ignoble. By its means I subordinate another human being to my own ends. In so doing I violate his or her dignity as a rational being. Such behavior is inconsistent, for again, I do not want to be on its receiving end. Thus the categorical imperative may be expressed by another and equivalent command. We must act so that we treat others *as ends in themselves* and never merely as a means.[4]

Yet moral action, thinks Kant, involves more than conformity to this law. To help others when we can, he explains, is a duty. There are also many minds "so sympathetically constituted" that they can take satisfaction in spreading joy around them.[5] We may enjoy such individuals, says Kant, and may regard them with affection. But it is a mistake, he believes, to attach moral worth to their actions. For their generosity, however amiable, proceeds not from respect for the moral law, but from their own nature.

---

[4] See p. 195.

[5] *Ibid.*, p. 160.

There are times, by contrast, when the choice is more difficult. Imagine that the mind of the philanthropist is "clouded by sorrows of his own," sorrows that extinguish his natural sympathy with others. Suppose now that he "tears himself out of this deadening insensibility," and performs the action, anyway. This action contains an element of will not present before. It is an element, thinks Kant, that bestows upon it a worth more profound than that of all the natural giving in the world.

Need an action involve this internal tug-of-war to merit respect? Does the natural good spirit of a free giver make his actions morally worthless?[6] Kant's view seems severe to many, yet in it we are reminded of the courage that it takes to do the right thing for the right reason. Those who have made this choice - as perhaps each of us has, at some time in life - can attest to the fact.

---

[6] Kant, it might be added, does not equate *moral character* across these cases. The man or woman who is above temptation may well be more highly evolved than is the other. (Compare, say, an individual who cannot think of child molestation with one who barely or only sometimes refrains from it.)

The Moral Law and the Material Universe

> Two things fill the mind with ever new and increasing admiration and awe, the oftener and more steadily we reflect upon them: the starry heavens above me and the moral law within me.
>
> Immanuel Kant, *Critique of Practical Reason*

There is no sight in nature more awesome, more astounding, than that of the heavens on a clear night. "The whole of our solar system," writes F. C. Happold,

> is only a minute part of the Milky Way, a galaxy of some ten million stars, across which it would take a hundred thousand light years to travel. The Milky Way is, moreover, only one of a literally countless number of galaxies, separated from each other by immeasurably vast stretches of inter-galactic space, each one made up of thousands of millions of stars.[7]

Can we do justice to this spectacle, at once majestic and frightening? The universe is too great, too fabulous, for our usual categories of thought. Its grandness is beyond description.

---

[7] F. C. Happold, *Mysticism: A Study and an Anthology* (London: Penguin Books, 1988), p. 22.

But just so, thinks Kant, it can overwhelm us, can make us feel as nothing by comparison. For what meaning can *we* have amidst this spectacle? How can we count, how can we matter, in this brief time and space, when we are as infinitesimal bits of sand in an endless sea?

Yet in us, Kant insists, is something no less impressive than the universe. Two things in all of experience, he writes, fill us with ever-new and increasing awe and admiration. There is the starry heaven I find looking out, and there is the moral law that speaks to me within.

The former "begins at the place I occupy in the external world of sense, and it broadens the connection in which I stand into an unbounded magnitude of worlds beyond worlds and systems of systems and into the limitless times of their periodic motion, their beginning and continuance."[8] The latter begins "at my invisible self," my soul, and it is infinite, as well.[9] In moral action I partake of something that has inestimable worth.

---

[8] Immanuel Kant, *Critique of Practical Reason*. Trans. Lewis White Beck (New York: The Liberal Arts Press, 1956), p. 166.

[9] *Ibid.* Kant, it might be added, is neither alone nor original in this observation. "Beneath you and external to you," writes the author of the earlier-mentioned book *The Cloud of Unknowing*, "lies the entire created universe. Yes, even the sun, the moon, and the stars. They are fixed above you, splendid in the firmament, yet they cannot compare to your exalted dignity as a human being." (p. 129)

The heavens may thus annihilate my importance as a material creature. But the moral law raises my worth in the same proportion. It reveals to me a life that is independent of my circumstance, a value and significance beyond estimate. This law cannot be judged upon any material scale, nor can the soul that is subject to it. Revealed to me in this law is a truth that is unconditional, as real and as vast as that given to my senses.

"Awe and admiration" - if the passage stirs in us a high feeling, its concern is down-to-earth. Basic and homely choices, day in and day out, are its province. Our choice of fairness toward others, our willingness to forego popular acceptance for principle - this is its issue.

If Kant is right, then we may need to rethink the ways in which we evaluate an individual human life. For the meaning of life, and the sum of our accomplishment, has nothing to do with the criteria that may often employ, such as fame or status. Nor has moral worth anything to do with moral reputation. Some of our most significant choices may be wholly inconspicuous. Actions of self-restraint, for example, can be invisible. A solitary exercise in self-examination, in truth, in fairness, may have no announcement. Kant reminds us that we are involved every day, even in private moments, in a struggle of supreme importance.

Truth Certain and Invisible

> As Plato said that the Good was "beyond existence" and Wordsworth that through virtue the stars were strong, so the Indian masters say that the gods themselves are born of the *Rta* and obey it. The Chinese also speak of a great thing ... called the *Tao*. It is the reality beyond all predicates, the abyss that was before the Creator Himself.
>
> C. S. Lewis, *The Abolition of Man*

Value, we sometimes hear, is outmoded in the face of *science*. The real things, it is said, are the ones that we can see and measure in the laboratory. Human behavior, on this line of reasoning, must be approached in these same terms. Notions of good and evil thus have no place in it, and belong to a older, less sophisticated phase of human understanding.

There is a increased tendency in the twentieth century, writes C. S. Lewis,[10] to suppose that value judgments can be reduced to facts of emotion. Our notions of what is good, what is noble or elevated, have no proof. Indeed they are not, on this view, statements at all, but mere reports of our own private feelings - or perhaps

---

[10] See especially parts I and II of *The Abolition of Man*.

not even reports, but just empty outpourings of empty noise. We must give greater attention to the structure of our language, say these analysts, and in so doing we will be able to cast away some of our traditional concerns. We will find that much philosophy is grounded in emotion. [11]

It is a fashionable view, says Lewis, but fact does not warrant it. Such a view is furthermore out of accord with our own deepest instinct. Across time and culture is the recognition of a source of value beyond all natural reckoning. While it bears different names, there is no mistaking its authority. The Chinese, call it the *Tao*. It is the way of reality and of life rightly lived.

The *Tao* is behind appearances. It does not come with rational guarantee. But if we take values seriously, says Lewis, we cannot do without it. If we truly believe that courage is better than cowardice, or kindness better than cruelty, we must suppose that there is more to reality than matter and motion. We must believe in the unseen.

---

[11] Such is the view, for example, of the *verificationists*, who hold that such judgments are neither true nor false, but are reducible to mere outbursts of feeling. This view, also called logical positivism, holds that all meaningful statements are either (1) "analytic," and state merely logical relations between ideas ("All squares are rectangles," "Eleven is a prime number," "Red things have color," etc.) or (2) "empirical," and so describe tangible states of affairs in the world (statements produced by the sciences, for example). So-called metaphysical claims - those that purport to go beyond the world of the senses - it thus deems void of content. For a classical statement, see A. J. Ayer, *Logic, Truth and Language* (New York: Dover Publications, 1952).

Some writers try to ground value instead in nature, explaining it in terms of our own evolutionary development. They do this, says Lewis, in the interest of progress, imagining that such an account is more in keeping with the modern awareness. Hence things like kindness and self-sacrifice, they maintain, are grounded in impulses acquired in our natural history. Such impulses convey no higher message, but reflect merely the impersonal accidents that have shaped our genetic structure.[12]

Yet how can impulse provide a basis for direction? Suppose, for example, that I have a biologically grounded wish to help others, or to promote freedom over tyranny. Should I obey it?

One may say that such an impulse is somehow higher or more mature than is some other. But *what fact of nature* can decide this? If I judge some impulses better, I must believe in the existence of real and objective principles that give this judgment its grounding. Only in going beyond nature, explains Lewis, can I find such a basis. Events in the molecular sphere cannot pass judgment upon themselves. For this reason, moral conviction leads us outside material bounds.

---

[12] For a current statement, see Robert Wright, *The Moral Animal* (New York: Vintage Books, 1994). I discuss this view at some length in *The Prospect of Immortality* (Draper, Utah: Homeward Bound Publishing, Inc., 1999).

A truth that is invisible? If this notion seems fanciful or soft-minded, it is not far removed from practical concerns. In order to see this, we might give attention to some of our own common-sense attitudes.

In what realm does value reside? Why, again, do we count some kinds of character, some kinds of behavior, as being higher and nobler than others? What is the point of defending an unpopular cause? Why do we want to instill certain notions of value in our sons and daughters? Some will say that we do these things because they are approved by society. But societies have approved many things, including slavery, that seem to have no objective worth today.

Nor does an explanation in terms of biology fare much better. My desire to help others, it is said, has its basis in my genes. But suppose that I have instead a genetically based impulse to commit random acts of violence on other people. Which of these natural tendencies should have my allegiance?

Some impulses, it seems, pull us in one direction, and some in another. In order to decide which to heed, I must stand outside this material situation and make my judgment on the basis of principle. The *Tao* is the reality, the timeless truth, in which a life must be grounded if it is to be sound.

VI

Causality and Freedom

One hears much about freedom. It serves, for example, as the chief rallying cry of many a social cause, where it signifies individual liberty in relation to the state. But there is another, more basic sense of freedom, one that concerns the depth structure of human action itself. It involves our potential for choice, our capacity for transcending the circumstances in which we reside. This primal freedom, or free agency, as we will soon note, is crucial to our thinking about value and responsibility.

Painting the Picture

> It is clearly understood that there is no definite painting to be made, that the artist is engaged in the making of his painting, and that the painting to be made is precisely the painting he will have made.
>
> Jean-Paul Sartre, "Existentialism"

Jean-Paul Sartre was part of a new wave of writers who emerged in the post-war years of Europe. They were, in the main, men and women who had borne grim witness to the conflict and had been decisively moved by the experience.

They were also rebels, writers with little use for standing notions of ethics and religion. Like many of this type, Sartre is an *existentialist* - he is a philosopher, in other words, who seeks to portray defining realities of the human condition. Thus his starting point is not abstract idea, but the concrete fact and challenge of this singular confrontation.[1]

---

[1] This movement, notes Eugene Borowitz, has as its foundation "the self, the concrete individual ... in a very specific here and now." It concerns "the jagged texture of concrete reality as against the clean contours of mental construction." See Eugene Borowitz, *A Layman's Introduction to Religious Existentialism* (Philadelphia: Westminster Press, 1965), p. 18.

Existentialism, like many terms in philosophy, has more than one meaning. In general terms, it is philosophy concerning human existence. For Sartre, it refers not only to an investigation of this event, but a set of definite theses concerning it. His essay "Existentialism"[2] is perhaps his best known and most accessible effort to frame its statement.

Central to Sartre's work is the element of agency. Much of his writing, both essay and drama, takes as its starting point the challenge that is posed to consciousness by its encounter with the world. It is a world, he tells us, that is outside and thus alien to ourselves. While he is an atheist, Sartre has something in common with philosophers in the spiritual tradition. He insists upon a radical difference between the self and the material world by which it is confronted. He insists likewise upon freedom as a fact of our existence. No fact, no set of outward circumstance, thinks Sartre, can decide our course of action. We are "condemned" to this fact, unable to escape it and with no real guideline for action.[3]

---

[2] Jean-Paul Sartre, *Existentialism*. Trans. Bernard Frechtman (New York: Philosophical Library, 1947).

[3] We can appeal to certain sources for guidance, but ultimately, insists Sartre, it is we who do the choosing. Thus the individual who consults, say, a priest for this purpose has already decided in advance the kind of advice that he or she will receive. There is a sense in which our choices precede our direction.

Who am I? What is my place in the scheme of things? Questions like these, thinks Sartre, have no answer prior to my own creative response to them. Whether I am, say, honest or dishonest, a hero or a coward, is fundamentally *up to me*. It is not decided by my natural constitution; it is not given to me, either, by the surrounding environment. It is instead my choice: In acting I create myself. My *existence*, which is to say, my bare reality as a free and conscious agent, precedes my *essence*, or the kind of creature that I am.

Sartre likens this self-forging process to the action of a painter. There is no rule telling the artist what to create, nor any blueprint showing how paintings in general ought to look. For this reason the product is truly his own. In like fashion, thinks Sartre, we shape ourselves by means of actions. Our life is in our hands. It will be, as yet, any number of things. We cannot, of course, decide all its circumstances, but we are free in relation to those circumstances that we may encounter. The painting will be what we make of it, unlike any other, and it will be as rich, as vibrant, as we choose.

The Hypothesis of an Open Universe

> In every outwardly verifiable and practical respect, a world in which the alternatives that actually now distract your choice were decided by pure chance would be by me absolutely undistinguished from the world in which I now live.
>
> William James, "The Dilemma of Determinism"

The classical problem of "free will" - do we really choose our actions, or are they effectively determined by the conditions into which we are born and by which we are surrounded?

This problem arises out of a collision of two rather ordinary beliefs. The first is that the world operates in accord with certain laws, certain regularities that govern the events within it. On this view, all that happens in the world is decided ultimately by the forces that operate through all of time with perfect regularity. The second is that the future is in some measure up to us, that it may yet contain one thing or another depending upon ourselves. On this latter view we have, as it were, an active say in things; the universe thus contains an element of novelty that it lacks otherwise. It is invested with a meaning that would be absent if genuine acts of will did not exist.

The first view is called *determinism*. It holds, says William James, that "those parts of the universe already laid down absolutely appoint and decree what the other parts shall be."[4] Given what has already happened, in other words, there is but one remaining causal "fit" - there is but one future allowed by the parts (the states of affairs, in other words) that have held until now. The world has no possibility "hidden in its womb" except this.

The second is *indeterminism*, the view containing, as James puts it, the element of *chance*. It allows that these parts have "a certain amount of loose play on one another, so that the laying down of one of them does not determine what the others shall be."[5]

On this latter view, then, the events that have lead up to this moment do not wholly decide what will come in the next. As things stand, the situation may yet unfold in one way or another, and a whole course of coming events may be different for it. Thus, for example, I may remain at this desk, or may get up and go for a walk. Of these eventualities (and perhaps others) now in mind's eye, one or another may transpire.

---

[4] William James, "The Dilemma of Determinism", contained in James' *The Will to Believe and other essays in popular philosophy* (New York: Dover Publications, 1956), p. 150. This book is bound together with James' *Human Immortality* as one volume.

[5] *Ibid.*

This issue, says James, has implications for our thinking about values. Consider, for one, our usual belief that we are responsible for our actions. We take it as a point of common sense, for example, that some things (say, cruelty, or gross injustice) are bad and ought not to be. We imagine that we are able, in some measure, to decide whether or not such things will come to pass. We thus feel that the moral condition of the world depends upon our own willful choices.

Yet if we suppose that determinism is true, thinks James, we will have a hard time maintaining these convictions. Consider for one, a peculiarly heinous act of murder. We count this a bad thing, something that ought not to happen, and that we are obliged to prevent if possible. Yet on the determinist account, this act is effectively guaranteed from the beginning, present from all of time in the causal chain. How, then, can it make sense to speak of the way things *might* or *should* have been?[6]

---

[6] Consider likewise, says James, our judgments of regret. If such judgments are ever appropriate, they surely are appropriate where gruesome violence is concerned. For anything, it seems, would be better in its place. If determinism is true, however, then this murder and nothing else must occupy this given portion of space and time. But in that case, *judgments of regret themselves* are inappropriate, and so something else ought to be in their place. But these judgments, according to the hypothesis, are as inevitable as the murder itself. Thus determinism, either way, seems to involve us in the assumption that something (whether the misdeed or our own reaction to it) inevitable should be otherwise. Hence the title of the essay.

Some, James observes, will say that we must accept determinism in any case. The notion of chance, they will claim, is irrational. For laws of science leave it no room. Yet science is founded on observation, and observation, says James, provides no warrant for the belief that our actions are determined.

Suppose, to cite a case, that I have the choice of walking home from the university hall by way of either Divinity Avenue or Oxford Street. Let us suppose that I take Divinity. Was this the only choice possible? Determinists will say so. But let us now imagine these ten minutes annihilated so that I am set back at the hall and faced with the choice again. This time I take Oxford. Having observed each sequence, can you say which was the real and necessary one?

If not, thinks James, you have no warrant, in the actual case, for interpreting this event (whichever way it unfolds) as being determined. Thus determinism, it seems, presupposes something not in evidence. We need not assume that our choices are determined, or that our lives are but cogs in some huge and aimless causal system. Perhaps our choices are real. Perhaps the universe indeed awaits our response.

Freedom and the Will to Meaning

> In the final analysis, the status drive or the will to power, on one hand, and the pleasure principle or, as one might term it as well, the will to pleasure, on the other hand, are mere derivatives of man's primary concern, that is, his will to meaning.
>
> Viktor Frankl, *The Will to Meaning*

There are theories, observes Viktor Frankl, that seek to reduce human beings to laws of material science. Such theories view their object as a kind of organic machinery, the helpless product, at bottom, of impersonal forces. Yet this view denies the basic fact of our own spirituality.

We have, says Frankl, certain capacities that resist explanation along mechanistic lines. One of these is our capacity for *self-detachment*. Consider, for one, our characteristic sense of humor. Likewise, our potential for heroism. These things require an ability to remove ourselves from our surroundings, to separate ourselves not only from outward circumstance, but from our existing frame of mind. In such cases we take a stand toward our own "somatic and psychic conditions" and all that surrounds us. We rise above such conditions and shape our own character.

We have likewise a capacity for *self-transcendence*. The most striking manifestations of this capacity, says Frankl, are love and conscience. Love enables me "to grasp the other human being in his very uniqueness." It allows me to have a relationship with another that is founded upon something more than impulse. Conscience, by the same token, empowers me "to seize the meaning of a situation in its very uniqueness." It enables me to address this situation in terms of its objective demands.

Our fundamental need, thinks Frankl, is not pleasure, or power, or any other such experiential commodity. It is instead *meaning* - an ideal for which we can stand, and which makes sense of the struggle in which we are involved. The psychiatry founded on this premise is called *logotherapy*, a treatment based upon the assumption that human life requires a *logos* or purpose no matter what else it may have.

Frankl returns to this theme in subsequent works. Only two classes of people, he writes, deny the basic freedom of the will - schizophrenic patients, who claim that their actions are controlled by others, and deterministic philosophers! We are not free from conditions, whether personal or environmental in nature. But we are free to take a stand toward them, to rise above their "plane" and to address our situation in terms of principle.

Deterministic theory claims that certain laws govern human behavior much as they govern inanimate nature. Yet his own experience in World War II concentration camps, Frankl explains, offered no confirmation of any such doctrine. During this time, he recalls, there was no identifiable fact or condition that determined the behavior of the prisoners. Decency and indecency continued to figure in the situation at every level, no matter how dire.[7] Thus while some individuals abandoned principle for a trifle or a food scrap, others would not abandon it for life itself.

We can set no limit, thinks Frankl, to what an individual may become over time. That one who is base, indecent, even thoroughly evil today, may be something more tomorrow. Such an individual, it is true, "will never be able to free himself from the ties which bind him to the various realms wherein he is confronted by unalterable conditions." But within such limits he is free, in crucially important ways, to take his stand.[8]

Frankl illustrates this by citing the conversation he had with an American psychoanalyst one Sunday morning in a coffeehouse in Vienna. On this occasion Frankl invited

---

[7] See Frankl's classic *Man's Search for Meaning* (New York: Washington Square Press, 1984).

[8] Viktor Frankl, *Psychotherapy and Existentialism* (New York: Simon and Schuster, 1967), pp. 59-60.

the man to join him on a mountain-climbing trip. The man refused, claiming that he had developed a deep aversion to such activity owing to the fact that his father had overextended him on such trips many years earlier. Now, recalls Frankl, "it was my turn to confess; and I began reporting to him that I, too, was taken on weekend trips by my father and hated them because they were fatiguing and annoying. But in spite of all that, I went on to become a climbing guide in an Alpine club." Conditions, he writes, never determine me; rather "I determine whether I yield to them."[9]

No set of circumstances, writes Frankl, can negate our freedom. Man does not behave according to what he is, but "also becomes what he is according to how he behaves. In the last analysis, man has become what he has made out of himself."[10] For this reason the individual personality "is essentially unpredictable." Sciences that have human behavior as their object must acknowledge our capacity "to emerge from and rise above all such conditions - to transcend them."

---

[9] *Ibid.*, p. 60.

[10] *Ibid.*, p. 61.

Freedom and Human Potential

> It is a serious thing to live in a society of possible gods and goddesses, to remember that the dullest and most uninteresting person you can talk to may one day be a creature which, if you saw it now, you would be strongly tempted to worship ...
>
> C. S. Lewis, "The Weight of Glory"

Freedom, as we have just seen, has implications for personal development. A free individual may change in ways that exceed expectation. He or she may change in ways that we cannot presently imagine. Nor, it seems, can we put any theoretical limit on the extent of this progress.

This issue of change and human potential arises as well in a religious context. Many of us, notes C. S. Lewis, put stock in the familiar idea that we and others are destined for a life beyond. Yet seldom do we bring this belief into alignment with their present outlook toward these same fellow journeyers

Consider the way that we exploit or subordinate others, how we dismiss them, at times, as being essentially inferior or unimportant in relation to ourselves. Think of the ways in which we seek to find some advantage over them in our daily operation.

At times, of course, our estimate is ill-founded. We may misjudge, or may employ foolish criteria in trying to decide how these individuals may stand. But ultimately, thinks Lewis, it makes no difference: Whatever this one's present condition, we must always acknowledge the possibility of his or her upward development.

Such an individual may undergo drastic change, of course, even within the span of this life. But when we extend the picture further, the prospect is staggering. Who knows what he or she may become with further opportunity? The least whom we meet today may be far more then, may indeed one day be unrecognizable from the creature who now stands before us.

What Lewis says about other people bears just as well upon ourselves. For we, too, may fail. In our guilt we may think that we are without hope. But in so doing we underestimate our prospects. If we are free, then we are never without the possibility of improvement. By our own action (and by God's grace, thinks Lewis), we may yet become something more. Our triumph over present limitation is thus a possibility both in this life and in the life to come.

Postulates of Moral Reason

> Man is certainly unholy enough, but humanity in his person must be holy to him. Everything in creation which he wishes and over which he has power can be used merely as a means; only man, and, with him, every rational creature, is an end in itself. He is the subject of the moral law which is holy, because of the autonomy of his freedom.
>
> Immanuel Kant, *Critique of Practical Reason*

We are subject, Kant maintains, to an unconditional moral law. This law is not an object of the senses - it cannot be seen or weighed as a material fact. But it is real. Our moral experience informs us a reality higher and greater than the one that the eyes disclose.

We are obliged, says Kant, to regard human beings as having a singular worth, to treat them as ends in their own right. If we accept this law as binding upon us, he maintains, then we must make room in our thought for certain other beliefs, as well. For one, we must believe ourselves to be free. For if we are subject to moral demand, then we must be capable of acting upon it. We cannot be bound by those laws that govern inanimate nature.

We must be able, says Kant, to act *on principle*. Within us must be a power that "elevates a man above himself as a part of the world of sense, something which connects him with an order of things which only the understanding can think and which has under it the entire world of sense."[11]

This law holds out to us moreover a certain ideal. This, says Kant, is *holiness*: the perfect conformity of our will to the moral law. It is an end that we, as moral agents, are required to achieve. But we are not capable of achieving it within this lifetime. (In fact, thinks Kant, we cannot reach it in any finite amount of time, in this world or any other.) Hence we are obliged to postulate - to suppose, in other words, for practical purposes - our own immortality. We must believe ourselves to be involved in a progress extending without limit beyond present limits.

Kant's discussion of moral experience and its bearing upon human destiny is an extraordinary chapter in the history of human thought. It a powerful influence upon philosophers to this day. This tie between ethics and religion is developed in the twentieth century by Hastings Rashdall in a two-volume work entitled *The Theory of Good and Evil*.

---

[11] Immanuel Kant, *Critique of Practical Reason*. Trans. Lewis White Beck (New York: The Liberal Arts Press, 1956), p. 89.

Our moral beliefs, says Rashdall, require from us certain assumptions about the universe in which we live. Not everyone, of course, explores this connection. Many of us have moral views and never stop to theorize about them. For this reason, says Rashdall, morality has a face-value independence from other issues. But when we begin to face facts, we find ourselves entering into *metaphysics* - into questions about the ultimate nature of reality. What we believe about good and evil has implications for such things as selfhood, freedom, and human destiny.

If we believe that we are responsible for our actions, then we must suppose that the self is a real and enduring thing - that it is more than some "mere accident or attribute or bye-product" of material forces. "It is a presupposition of all Morality," writes Rashdall, "that the self is the cause of its own actions."[12] Our recognition of good and evil presupposes likewise their real existence.

We believe, too, "that the Moral Law has a real existence, that there is something absolutely true or false in ethical judgements, whether we or any number of human beings at any given time actually think so or not."[13]

---

[12] Hastings Rashdall, *The Theory of Good and Evil* (Oxford: Clarendon Press, 1907), Volume II, p. 200.

[13] *Ibid.*, p. 211. While this belief, of course, is not universal, some human beings, contends Rashdall, perceive its truth.

The question remains as to where such a law resides. It cannot, says Rashdall, exist in material things. It must instead reside in a mind - not a mind, like ours, of singular vantage point, but one without limit. It must be a mind not merely of idea, but of will. If our own moral voice is a reflection of this source, it must present to us "the nature of the end toward which that Reality is moving."[14]

What end might this be? This world, thinks Rashdall, cannot be its completion. Can anyone, he asks, believe that the world, in its present condition, "is so good as to account for its having been willed by a perfectly good and perfectly rational Being, except as a means to an end beyond itself?" Justice is not accomplished here. In which case, the end at which this world aims must lie ahead. It must involve our own continued participation if it expresses the higher will that is revealed by our own moral experience.

---

[14] *Ibid.*, p. 213.

VII

Beauty

What sort of thing is *beauty*? Surely it is desirable, and few things are sought after more than beauty of appearance and possessions. But while it is desirable, it is also, say some, a superficial good. For it varies with personal taste, and so it lacks an objective basis.

Is this view correct? Certainly it is common. But it is not universal. The final *desideratum*, it has been said, consists in truth, goodness, and beauty.[1] *The beautiful*, Plato maintains, is eternal. All mortal knowledge, says Keats, comes to the realization that truth and beauty are one. To such ideas we now turn.

---

[1] These three, writes Mortimer Adler, are the principal ideas by which we judge, just as liberty, equality, and justice are those by which we act. See Adler's *Six Great Ideas* (New York: Macmillan, 1981). At times it is said that they are really the same thing. In the thought of the Earl of Shaftesbury, writes Terry Eagleton, "what is beautiful is harmonious, what is harmonious is true, and what is at once true and beautiful is agreeable and good." See Eagleton's *The Ideology of the Aesthetic* (Oxford: Basil Blackwell, 1990), p. 35.

Legacy of the Greeks

> The Greek pursues beauty and goodness as things that are identical or at least always coincident; in fact he gives them a single name, the beautiful-and-good, *to kalo-kagathia*.
>
> William Barrett, *Irrational Man*

Our civilization, writes William Barrett, is a product of two divergent civilizations, those of the Hebrews and the Greeks.[2] From the first we get *the law*; from it we inherit, in other words, our consciousness of a valid and unconditional claim upon our lives. From the second we get *the ideal of rationality*.

The first of these elements involves commitment. The second, by contrast, involves detachment. Its product is *theory*, deduction, objective reason. In theoretical activity we maintain our distance, beholding the world much as we behold performance on the stage.[3]

---

[2] Barrett begins his discussion by quoting from Matthew Arnold's nineteenth century work *Culture and Anarchy*. See pp. 69 and following of the earlier-cited book *Irrational Man*.

[3] Thus again, as we have seen, there is blood tie between such words as 'theory', 'theater', and 'aesthetic', each in some way connoting personal distance.

Such an ideal, explains Barrett, is unlike that of our other cultural root. It issues from an untroubled soul, one at ease in the face of eternity. In Athens one finds not the biblical fear of God or the related consciousness of sin, but "the ... luminous play of the intelligence." This intelligence gives rise to abstract geometry and aerial achievement in shape and architecture.

In Greece, writes Andrew Harvey, is a wondrous blend of "depth, daring, variety, and richness."[4] In Plato is one example. Centuries later, one finds in the like-spirited philosopher Plotinus a universe "everywhere radiant with the presence of divine beauty." It is a beauty, says Harvey, "that waits only for the soul to be purified to reveal itself in all its wounding, ecstatic loveliness."[5] The world, writes Plotinus, is a majestic organism, minutest part related to whole, artistry evident in such tiny portions that "you would not have thought that Providence would bother about them."[6]

---

[4] Andrew Harvey, ed., *The Essential Mystics* (San Francisco: HarperCollins, 1997). See chapter 6, "Ancient Greece: The Way of Beauty".

[5] *Ibid.*, p. 112.

[6] *Ibid.*, p. 130. This and related excerpts from Plotinus' *Enneads* are cited by Harvey in pp. 129-35.

Truth and Reflection

> Is the man who holds that there are fair things but doesn't hold that there is beauty itself, and who, if someone leads him to the knowledge of it, isn't able to follow - is he, in your opinion, living in a dream or is he awake?
>
> Socrates, Plato's *Republic*

We are familiar today with the old saw that beauty lies in the eye of the beholder. Such an attitude, we may imagine, is the proper one, extending respect to all tastes in a spirit of charity. Better, we may think, to level all ideas than to pass judgment on any of them.

This "eye of the beholder" view, as we have noted, has found an audience in both ancient times and present. There is no truth, it holds, beyond truth-as-it-seems, no value but what we happen to enjoy. Perhaps its appeal owes to the fact that it makes life easier - that it releases us from the task of examination. If beauty, after all, is only a matter of preference, then there is no need to explore the situation further. My taste cannot be inferior, or poorly developed, if each taste is equal to every other. I have no need to make more of myself, in this regard, if no truth exists outside immediate experience.

Such an outlook, again, is common. But what is the alternative? Some thinkers have held instead that beauty is a real thing, *a thing unto itself* to be known and appreciated as an independent fact. It is, Plato tells us, a sacred thing, apprehended in stages as our own maturation allows. An awareness of beauty, he maintains, is basic to our understanding of truth. The process is described by Socrates, who cites the words of his own teacher Diotima. The true learner, she explains, climbs a ladder

> from bodily beauty to the beauty of institutions, from institutions to learning, and from learning in general to the special lore that pertains to nothing but the beautiful itself - until at last he comes to know what beauty is.[7]

We first admire beauty in some singular and physical instance. Soon our appreciation widens. In time we find beauty of another order, one more rarefied, such as that inhering in rational principle.

Our understanding proceeds with our growth. Eventually we see a beauty that transcends the material world altogether. Thus we see the beauty of the soul, surpassing what is discerned by the outward senses. Ultimately, says Diotima, we behold an ultimate truth, Beauty itself, beyond time and suffering no imperfection.

---

[7] *Symposium* 211c. (Hamilton and Cairns.)

This view is reiterated by a number of writers in recent times. Value, maintains C. S. Lewis, is an essential part of reality. For this reason it is also an essential part of our understanding. Real education, Lewis explains, will train us in the appreciation of beauty as well as in the appreciation of history and mathematics. Our abandonment of value is tantamount to spiritual suicide.[8] If we are to apprehend the truth, we must be trained in both mind and spirit.

If we are to become fully human, we must understand, for example, the difference between noble and ignoble behavior. We must understand likewise that reality has an aesthetic dimension. There is a crucial difference between good literature and bad, between high and low accomplishment in the arts. The worth of a thing is not measured, as some imagine, by our enjoyment of it. Rather the fact precedes the feeling. Our fundamental virtue might thus be called *ordo amoris*, an affection for each thing according to its objective worth.[9] Nor is every positive adjective appropriate to a valuable thing. (It will not do, for example, to call a waterfall *pretty* when it is really more.)

---

[8] See again *The Abolition of Man*.

[9] See pp. 28-29. Lewis cites discussion by St. Augustine in *The City of God*, Book XV, chapter 22 and elsewhere.

Again, it is an old idea. In the later Greek tradition is Plotinus. There is, writes this disciple of Plato, a principle that bestows beauty upon material things. The soul has a faculty addressing this truth, recognizing it "as from an ancient knowledge," and so welcoming it. Seeing this element, the soul "thrills with an immediate delight, takes its own to itself, and thus stirs anew to the sense of its nature and of all its affinity."[10]

Outward perception may provide its first occasion. But the soul will discover "earlier and loftier" examples that exceed this range.[11] To such heights we must ultimately rise.

Not all are capable of the task. Some are excluded from it as the blind are excluded from the joys of sight. Those with understanding realize that there is beauty not only of physical appearance, but of conduct and discernment. They behold the splendor of virtue, and "the Face of Justice and of Moral-Wisdom beautiful beyond the beauty of Evening and of Dawn."

Such vision is for those "with the Soul's sight." At this vision "they will rejoice, and awe will fall upon them and a trouble deeper than all the rest could ever stir, for now they are moving in the Realm of Truth."

---

[10] Enneads, cited in *The Essential Mystics.*, p. 130.

[11] *Ibid.*, p. 132.

This vision brings "longing and love and a trembling that is all delight." To those fitted to see it, this great unseen is self-evident. Indeed every soul does gain some intimation of its truth, though not with such impact; by analogy, says Plotinus, "all take delight in the beauty of the body but all are not stung as sharply, and those only that feel the keener wound are known as Lovers."[12]

---

[12] *Ibid.*

A Famous Ode

> "Beauty is Truth, truth beauty," - that is all Ye know on earth, and all ye need to know.
>
> John Keats, "Ode on a Grecian Urn"

It has captured our imagination since it was written more than one hundred seventy-five years ago. Much has been said as to its meaning. Does the statement convey literal truth? Does it merely express instead some passing flight of emotion?

There is a popular tendency, once again, to think of beauty as being something pleasant, as being something that entertains us and arouses our desires. Keats takes us further. For in apprehending beauty, he realized, we are not merely entertained, but elevated. It was his "yearning passion for the beautiful," writes one commentator, "that held the young poet steadily to his course."[13] Keats, he explains, apprehends a beauty "that far transcends sensuous loveliness; it is rooted in an intuitive knowledge of the human heart and the spiritual laws of life."

---

[13] Clarence D. Thorpe, *The Mind of John Keats* (New York: Oxford University Press, 1926), p. 127.

The conception of beauty as something beyond nature finds expression in recent Christian thought. Beauty, writes J. B. Phillips, seems to be "a pointer to something ... beyond the present limits of time and space."[14] It thus carries the intimation of a greater reality.

Keats' poem is itself timeless. In it rings the truth of Greek thought at its apex - that *beauty gives insight* into the universe. In beauty we are not merely pleased or given diversion. We are made aware of the ultimate truth in all of life.[15] These days we are inclined to associate objectivity with coldness and neutrality. What Keats understands, fully in the spirit of Athens, is that truth is aligned not with these things, but with splendor, with beauty, with the most elevated and joyous moments of our existence.

---

[14] J. B. Phillips, *Your God is Too Small* (New York: Collier Books, 1961), p. 70.

[15] Real beauty, claims Thorpe, "is of the everlasting reality that lies behind the mere surface and seeming of earthly things." While he does not push too far the comparison of Keats with Plato, he sees their affinity. Whoever can grasp beauty "has laid hold of permanent, indestructible truth; he has enjoyed, moreover, the highest type of aesthetic experience - he has known Beauty face to face." (p. 158) Cf. chapter 17, "The Goodness of Beauty and the Beauty of Truth", in Adler's *Six Great Ideas*. See also Hans-Georg Gadamer, *The Relevance of the Beautiful and other essays* (Cambridge: Cambridge University Press, 1986).

The Beautiful and the Sublime

> Finer feeling, which we now wish to consider, is chiefly of two kinds: the feeling of the *sublime* and that of the *beautiful*. The stirring of each is pleasant, but in different ways.
>
> Immanuel Kant,
> *Observations on the Feeling of the Sublime and the Beautiful*

We give little thought these days to "finer feelings." In this passage, reminiscent of the literature of the Greeks, Kant bids us to study them more closely. Our aesthetic experience, he observes, involves us not merely in an apprehension of *the beautiful*, but of *the sublime*.

We find the former in "the sight of flower-strewn meadows, valleys with winding brooks and covered with grazing flocks." The latter, by contrast, may reside in "a mountain whose snow-covered peak rises above the clouds, the description of a raging storm, or Milton's portrayal of the infernal kingdom."[16]

---

[16] Immanuel Kant, *Observations on the Feeling of the Beautiful and Sublime*. Trans. John T. Goldthwait (Berkeley: University of California Press, 1991), p. 47.

This latter apprehension involves a subtler feeling; it is aligned more with depth and with mystery. "Tall oaks and lonely shadows in a sacred grove are sublime; flower beds and trees trimmed in figures are beautiful."

> Night is sublime, day is beautiful. Temperaments that possess a feeling for the sublime are drawn gradually, by the quiet stillness of a summer evening as the shimmering light of the stars breaks through the brown shadows of night and the lonely moon rises into view, into high feelings of friendship, of disdain for the world, of eternity.[17]

Our sense of the sublime is connected, thinks Kant, to our moral awareness. While some ascribe sublimity to God, or to the highest human genius,[18] we find it present also in human dignity. True virtue consists in "the *feeling of the beauty and the dignity of human nature*."[19] If the first of these is the ground of our affection, the second is the ground of our esteem.

---

[17] *Ibid.*

[18] See references to Shaftesbury, Mendelssohn, and others in the translator's introduction, pp. 23 and following.

[19] *Observations*, p. 60. This discussion, it might be noted, belongs to a relatively early and "pre-critical" period in Kant's writings before he began to address himself, in a highly technical style, to various problems of knowledge and metaphysics. The account of virtue here is different from later ones (noted in chapter 2), in which Kant explains this quality not in terms of feeling, but of choice. Nonetheless Kant's apprehension of human dignity figures prominently each account.

Inspiration

> You do not know what is in you - an inexhaustible fountain of ideas.
>
> Brenda Ueland, *If You Want to Write*

Brenda Ueland was born in Minneapolis in 1891. For much of her life she was a writer, editor, and teacher of writing, and she lived an active and vital life until her passing at 93 in 1985. Her book *If You Want to Write* is a classic of instruction and encouragement to aspiring writers.

In reading this book one may envy Ueland's students for what was surely one of the most valuable experiences of their lives. Her courses were quite different in their focus from those of the more conventional kind. They had in them little, for one, of nitpicking or textbook criticism. For what students needed more, she believed, was a break from unhealthy inhibition that until now had dammed up their innate ability. To this end, she sought to bring out of students what was present at their core depths. In them, she was convinced, was latent genius awaiting its chance. Real creation requires not endless practice in rule and regulation, but release.

The writer who trusts instinct, says Ueland, will find success.[20] Her book, which had its first printing in 1938, features chapters like "Be careless, reckless! Be a lion, be a pirate, when you write"; "Keep a slovenly, headlong, impulsive, honest diary"; and "Why women who do too much housework should neglect it for their writing".

Ueland's own spirit flows like vital current through her own work. Time and again she returns to the theme of *inspiration*, of that endless fountain of truth present in oneself: Once making the commitment and heeding the truth, we will not lack for ideas. The book is as much a statement on religion as on writing, and in reading it one sees that the two are not altogether separate.

The greatest poets speak from the depths of the soul. In their words truth crystallizes in sheer simplicity. "My heart leaps up," writes William Wordsworth, on beholding a rainbow in the sky.[21] Here is voiced the undying wisdom of the child who sees nature's own presage of heaven.

---

[20] For every pupil, C. S. Lewis reminds us, "who needs to be guarded from a weak excess of sensibility there are three who need to be awakened from the slumber of cold vulgarity." The task of a modern educator, he adds, "is not to cut down jungles but to irrigate deserts." (*Abolition of Man*, p. 27)

[21] See Wordsworth's "My heart leaps up when I behold", contained in John O. Hayden, ed., *William Wordsworth: Selected Poems* (London: Penguin Books, 1994), p. 138.

He who plants a tree, says Lucy Larcom, plants a hope.[22] As its leaves unfold into free horizons, so do we climb to greater heavens, as yet unaware, at our root level, of the glory awaiting.

In the words of such individuals is a vision of reality beyond the pale. "Life, like a dome of many colored glass," declares Shelley, "Stains the white radiance of eternity."[23] So, he sees, does the timeless soul now shine through its mortal prism.

Artists of all kinds bear witness to creative inspiration. In the second chapter of his book *The Personality of Man*, G. N. M. Tyrrell cites the testimony of renowned writers and lyricists.[24] "The songs," says Goethe, "made me; not I them"; "I ... write every scene down at once," reports Dostoevsky, "as it first comes to me and rejoice in it; then I work at it for months and years."[25]

---

[22] Lucy Larcom, "Plant a Tree", contained in Roy J. Cook, ed., *One Hundred and One Famous Poems* (Chicago: Contemporary Books, 1958).

[23] See Shelley's "Adonais", written in memory of John Keats, reprinted often and contained in G. B. Harrison, ed., *A Book of English Poetry* (London: Penguin Books, 1950).

[24] G. N. M. Tyrrell, *The Personality of Man* (Middlesex: Penguin Books Ltd., 1947). See chapter 2, "Inspiration and Genius".

[25] *Ibid.*, pp. 32-33. Cf. Harry Emerson Fosdick, *On Being a Real Person* (New York: Harper and Brothers, Publishers, 1943).

Here again, we may note, modern insight is anticipated by the Greek. The talent of reciting Homer, writes Plato, "is a power divine."[26] It is not the result of mere study or applied conscious effort, but a gift from beyond.

Like the magnet that attracts an iron ring and imparts its own power, just so the Muse. She first makes certain men inspired, and through them, others in turn. The real lyric poets are not in their senses; launching into their rhythm, "they are seized with the Bacchic transport and are possessed." A poet, says Plato, is "a light and winged thing, and holy, and never able to compose until he has become inspired, and is beside himself, and reason is no longer in him."

Plato returns to this theme in the *Phaedrus*, in which he describes a special madness inspiring the priestesses of the oracles. The greatest blessings come by way of this force that "seizes a tender, virgin soul and stimulates it to rapt passionate expression ... glorifying the countless mighty deeds of ancient times."[27] Should any man come to this arena thinking that mere skill will make him a poet, he will be brought to nothing.

---

[26] See *Ion* 533d and following. (Hamilton and Cairns)

[27] See *Phaedrus* 244a and following. (Hamilton and Cairns)

If we are to write, thinks Ueland, we must trust ourselves. We must not become so preoccupied with rule and regulation that we fail to express what is within us. Writing, she insists further, has an intrinsic reward, and no writing is a waste of time: "With every sentence you write, you have learned something. It has done you good. It has stretched your understanding."

... and all manner of thing shall be well.

VIII

Mystic Voices

At the heart of life is a question. "Shall the seen world or the unseen world," asks William James in his great classic, "be our chief sphere of adaptation?"[1] Which world, in other words, has our allegiance?

Previous chapters have shown how our views regarding such things as value, freedom, and obligation may extend our world-view outside the bounds of the natural sphere. This chapter and the two following focus upon the question of higher realities and their relationship to our present life activity.

---

[1] William James, *The Varieties of Religious Experience* (New York: Macmillan Books, 1961), p. 295. This material was given in substance by James in his Gifford Lectures at the University of Edinburgh at the turn of the century.

The Point of Departure

> The most highly developed branches of the human family have in common one peculiar characteristic. They tend to produce - sporadically it is true, and often in the teeth of adverse external circumstances - a curious and definite type of personality; a type which refuses to be satisfied with that which other men call experience, and is inclined, in the words of its enemies, to "deny the world in order that it may find reality."
>
> Evelyn Underhill, *Mysticism*

In every age, as Evelyn Underhill observes, there are some who find their highest truth outside the bounds of this world. The present life, they tell us, is but a passing phase. For there is more to reality, more to our own deeper nature, than meets the eye.

The word 'mysticism' signals a departure from the things that surround us. Akin to 'mystery', it has the same soft feel, rather like a shroud or phantom. Its Greek ancestor, notes one contemporary author,[2] is *mustikos*, a term conveying secrecy, and *muein*, a closing of the eyes or mouth associated with hidden rite.

---

[2] See Dennis Tamburello, *Ordinary Mysticism* (New York: Paulist Press, 1996).

There are some types, firmly rooted in this world, who greet such ideas with suspicion. Thus the mystic label, in some quarters, implies fraud or imbalance. But this is not its primary meaning. Nor is any such characterization of the mystic personality warranted. Those who see other worlds, as a rule, do not lack for good sense in this one.

What is a mystical experience like? It is not, we are told, an intellectual event. Instead it is sudden, intuitive, like unto a flash. It has, writes William James in his great work *The Varieties of Religious Experience*, four essential characteristics; these are *ineffability*, *noetic quality*, *transiency*, and *passivity*.[3]

The mystical state is ineffable, writes James, in that "no adequate report can be given of its contents." One can talk about it, perhaps offer a hint through image or logical comparison. But its substance must be known firsthand Thus it is better classed, says James, as a state of feeling than as one of intellect. It is transient, lasting typically only a few moments, and passive, for "when the characteristic sort of consciousness has set in, the mystic feels as if his own will were in abeyance, and indeed sometimes as if he were grasped and held by a superior power."

---

[3] See *The Varieties of Religious Experience*, pp. 299-300.

And it is noetic. The meaning of this word may be gleaned from its Greek ancestor *nous*, which means mind or intelligence. A noetic thing is thus informative. The visions and raptures of the mystic, it seems, are not mere departures from normality. They tell us something about *the nature of reality*.

Mystical experiences may effect whole conversions of attitude and life-outlook.[4] They also convey a supernatural insight. This fact can be put in perspective by the testimony of St. Thomas Aquinas, the principal philosopher of the middle ages. Thomas wrote treatises on ethics and theology that remain essential reading in many of today's programs. Near the end of his life, he had a vision so revealing that his own writings, he felt, were like straw by comparison.[5]

---

[4] The so-called near-death experience, much cited in recent years, provides illustration. See, for example, Ray Moody, Jr.'s classic *Life After Life* (New York: Bantam Books, 1975). "I want to do things because they are good," reports one subject, "not because they are good to me. And it seems that the understanding I have of things now is so much better." (p. 90) After the experience, says another, "many have remarked to me that I seem to have almost a calming effect on them, instantly, when they are troubled." (pp. 91-92)

[5] This remark is noted by E. L. Miller in his *God and Reason* (Englewood Cliffs, New Jersey: Prentice-Hall, 1995), p. 107. See also discussion in Robert Barron, *Thomas Aquinas - Spiritual Master* (New York: Crossroad Publishing Company, 1996).

Our Real Identity

> ... since man is contained in space-time phenomena, he does not easily perceive the real nature of the world or of himself. He imagines he is wholly bound up with his ephemeral, phenomenal self. He does not easily perceive that his true self is of that changeless Spirit, with which it is, of its nature, one.
>
> F. C. Happold,
> *Mysticism: A Study and an Anthology*

Mysticism is the blood, the energizing force, of all religion. From its tradition, observes F. C. Happold, we find testimony, east and west, to a greater self, profound and enduring, hidden like the mass of an iceberg beneath the surface.

The lore of India abounds in such claims. The ancient *Upanishads* (classic treatises devoted to spiritual development) tell of a young boy who leaves home to study under a master and returns years later full of pride.[6]

---

[6] *Chandogya* Upanishad, Part 6. For text and commentary, see Swami Prabhavananda, *The Spiritual Heritage of India* (Hollywood: Vedanta Press, 1980), pp. 55 and following. See also volume 4 of Swami Nikhilananda's translation of the *Upanishads* (New York: Ramakrishna-Vivekananda Center, 1959).

Is he wise? Does he know, asks his father, that subtle truth "by which we hear the unhearable, perceive the unperceivable, and know the unknowable"? Time and again he is directed away from his own self-confining nature, to look at things great and small, things visible and invisible. Look higher, he is told - *Thou art that*. His real nature is without limit.

In looking out, writes Swami Prabhavananda, the ancient seers saw a world in motion. So, too, when they looked within. The mind was a flood of incessant change - thoughts, fancies, images, and feelings, "like restless waves upon a shoreless sea." But there was more. Behind these waves, superior to them, was *atman*, "a silent and constant witness" to the passing scene.

Knowledge of this greater self is not gained by cleverness or scholarship. It is a spiritual event - "by him who longs for him is he known."[7] The true self is "omniscient Lord."[8] *Brahman*, the limitless truth - "That art thou." Our own true nature is greater, more conscious, more blissful, than we yet realize.

---

[7] This passage (*Mundaka* Upanishad, Part 3) is quoted by Prabhavananda in chapter 3.

[8] *Katha* Upanishad, Part 1.

The Ultimate Promise

> If we were to take Hinduism as a whole - its vast literature, its complicated rituals, its sprawling folkways, its opulent art - and compress it into a single affirmation, we would find it saying: You can have what you want.
>
> Huston Smith, *The World's Religions*

It is indeed quite a promise. One can miss its full impact. What, after all, *do* we want?

Many smile at the thought of "heaven." Who, they ask, wishes to sit upon clouds, strumming soft tunes, idling away time in such odd and empty fashion? The joys of this life, by contrast, are concrete and knowable. What others can there be?

But let us give free rein, for a moment, to desire. What, asks Huston Smith, do we *really* want? This is not a question about what we want at this moment, or at some phase of life. It requires an exercise of the imagination.

Classical Indian society, as noted in an earlier chapter, divides individual human types (and thus society as well) into four principal classes. It also recognizes four levels of basic fulfillment corresponding to levels of individual growth. These are *kama* (pleasure), *artha* (success), *dharma* (duty), and *moksha* (liberation). They are stages not merely of a single lifetime, but of a journey that can span many rounds.

In *moksha*, say the *Upanishads*, is freedom.[9] No rule fixes our rate of progress toward this goal. But we are ultimately driven to it by our own nature. For no end prior to this fully satisfying. No other end speaks to what is contained in our potential. Thus pleasure, for example, may occupy us for a time, but it cannot satisfy us indefinitely. The same is true of the further material victories of wealth, fame, or power. Our needs rise with our own development.[10]

Where, then, are we headed? In order to see the extent of the Vedic promise, we might think for a moment in terms more familiar. Suppose that we ask a five-year old his fondest desire. A toy, a visit to an amusement park - in a typical case, it might be nothing that lasted beyond a matter of hours. The answer to this question 12 years later will be more sophisticated, but with limits just as obvious. It will express the wants of a nature that is conditioned by a specfic level of growth and awareness.

---

[9] See, for example, *Mundaka* Part 3.

[10] A parallel wisdom may be found in the west. The aesthetic attitude, writes Barrett in a kindred vein, "can only be a partial, never a complete, attitude toward life." In time it must collapse into despair. See *Irrational Man*, pp. 163 and following.

The answer in twenty more years will show advancement, but it will bear the same marks. Let us then ask the question in a more abstract vein, forgetting limitation altogether. What would be *the wisest answer possible* from outside these developmental bounds?

What we want at base, thinks Smith, are three things. These are (1) being, (2) awareness, and (3) happiness.[11] We want these things furthermore *without limit*. What we want, if we think without restraint, is life unrestricted to its present few decades; we want knowledge, not in finite measure, but whole and complete. And we want happiness. This present happiness that we now enjoy is a precarious thing, dependent upon circumstance. The one that we want exceeds, in its extent and quality, the one with which we are familiar.

We are now in a position to see the wondrousness of the claim. The very greatest moments of this life - its achievements, glories, and acquisitions - are as nothing to what is really ours. We are, say the scriptures, like men and women wandering the world for treasure with gold just under our feet. *Atman* and *Brahman* are one: The good that we can scarcely imagine is destined to be ours.

---

[11] These are known respectively in the Sanskrit as *sat*, *chit*, and *ananda*.

Our Inseparability from Home

> And as the Deity, Father, Son, and Holy Spirit are always in Heaven and make Heaven to be everywhere, so this Spirit, breathed by them into man, brought Heaven into man along with it; and so man was in Heaven as well as on earth; that is, in Paradise, which signifies an heavenly state or birth of life.
>
> William Law, *The Spirit of Prayer*

Eternity, we imagine, is yet to come. Ultimate reality, it seems, is something distant. Our frame of mind regarding these things blinds us to their immediacy.

In fact, we live in eternity already. Our immortality is something that enjoy now just as we will (though perhaps in grander fashion) hereafter. As God's creation, we are an expression, at this moment, of His nature.

Heaven, writes William Law, is as close to our souls as this world is to our bodies. God is not distant; if He seems so, it is because we lack the spirit of prayer that cannot fail to unite us "with the One only Good, and to open Heaven and the kingdom of God within us."[12]

---

[12] This portion of Law's work *The Spirit of Prayer* is reprinted in F. C. Happold's *Mysticism - A Study and an Anthology* (London: Penguin Books, 1988), pp. 377-83.

In each of us is a flame that overcomes ill and generates the life of heaven. If we fail to see God, it is because we use only our exterior senses. We make our search "in books, in controversies, in the church and outward exercises" - everywhere but where He dwells! He is present in the deepest part of ourselves. The outward senses cannot possess God or unite Him with us; nor indeed can the inward faculties of will or understanding. But there is a root in us, Law writes, "from whence all these faculties come forth, as lines from a centre or as branches from the body of the tree."

This depth is the unity, the infinity of the soul, by which we are united with something that has no limit. Within us, by supernatural gift, is a spark whose ceaseless tendency is to reach for the light from which it came. "Begin to search and dig in thine own field," says Law, "for this pearl of eternity that lies hidden in it." In finding it, "thou wilt know that all which thou hast sold or given away for it is ... as a bubble upon the water."[13]

---

[13] *Ibid.*, p. 380.

An Apprehension of Ultimate Reality

> ... in the world of knowledge the idea of good appears last of all, and is seen only with an effort; and, when seen, is also inferred to be the universal author of all things beautiful and right, parent of light and of the lord of light in this visible world, and the immediate source of reason and truth in the intellectual; and that this is the power upon which he who would act rationally either in public or private life must have his eye fixed.
>
> Socrates, Plato's *Republic*

This passage, which comes in Book VII of Plato's *Republic*, has excited fascination from the time of its origin. In it is a vision of all that is real, and of the sovereign truth of goodness as a first and guiding principle.

Plato, as we have seen, divides reality into two realms, one that is passing and one that is permanent. The latter of these is our true home and destiny. We today tend to think of reality in a kind of all or nothing fashion. Yet for Plato it has an order, an ascending scale, according to worth.[14]

---

[14] This so-called divided line of reality is illustrated and described in Book VI, section 509e and following. (Hamilton and Cairns)

Within each realm is an order. In the sensible world, there are tangible objects and the images cast by them. The images derive their reality from these objects, and so have a lower place in the scheme. But image and object alike belong to the realm of the visible. There is another world beyond them.

In this higher world, as we have noted in a previous chapter, are things eternal. They are immaterial things - the objects, for example, of mathematics, which include numbers and essential geometric shapes. Above these are entities still greater, the *forms*, as Plato calls them, such as *wisdom* and *justice*. Highest is *the Good*, like unto the sun, reigning over all, illuminating reality and giving birth to truth and intelligence.

Plato's description of the Good is counted as one of the world's great philosophical passages. It is surely one of the most exciting. In it we are told the first principle of all reality - that the universe is ultimately a good thing. It is not evil, as writers like Bertrand Russell have imagined.[15] Nor is it some huge and meaningless eternal void. Instead, reality is a place in which truth and goodness converge. We are at home.

---

[15] The world may have no purpose, says Russell, but if it has one, it must be the purpose of a fiend. See "Do We Survive Death?", reprinted in his book *Why I Am Not a Christian* (New York: Simon and Schuster, 1957).

This conviction is not unique to Athens. The Vedic tradition, as we have seen, holds something kindred. Listen also to the twentieth century voice of A. M. Greeley. Life, writes Greeley, "seems most of the time to be absurd, capricious, random - and occasionally downright ugly and vindictive."[16] There are times when we are tempted to write if off as something quite senseless. Yet our hope is not quite extinguished.

We are born with two diseases - one is life, from which we die, and the other is a hope that tells us that life is not futile. We are left to wonder which perception - that of life's absurdity, or that of its greater meaning - is correct. Perhaps our optimism is a cruel joke played upon us by nature. But the message of Jesus, says Greeley, is that hope is to be *trusted*. It is to be treated as an intimation of truth. And still, it does not go far enough: "In effect, Jesus said, hope your wildest hopes, dream your maddest dreams, imagine your most fantastic fantasies. Where your hopes and your dreams and your imagination leave off, the love of my heavenly Father only begins."

---

[16] This article, entitled "A Christmas Biography", appeared in *The New York Times Magazine* of December 23, 1973, pp. 28-30. It is excerpted in Brian Tierney, Donald Kagan, and L. Pearce Williams, eds., *Great Issues in Western Civilization* (New York: McGraw-Hill, Inc., 1992).

The Story of the Universe in a Single Sentence

> He shewed me a little thing, the quantity of an hazel-nut, in the palm of my hand; and it was as round as a ball. I looked thereupon with eye of my understanding, and thought: What may this be? And it was answered generally thus: It is all that is made.
>
> Julian of Norwich, *Revelations of Divine Love*

Greeley's message is presaged by that of a young peasant girl who lived in the region of Norfolk, England, in the fourteenth century. As biographer Elizabeth Obbard notes,[17] the girl's birth was an obscure event. She entered the world, in all likelihood, amidst crowded city streets, and we do not know her parentage or baptismal name. We call her by her acquired name of Julian.

We speak today of hard times. But they are nothing like hers. The black plague entered the area when Julian was six, bringing death and living hell in its wake - "men and women could rise in the morning feeling healthy and be dead by evening, their faces bloated, their bodies already near decomposition." The plague, Obbard explains,

---

[17] Elizabeth Ruth Obbard, *Introducing Julian - Woman of Norwich* (Hyde Park: New City Press, 1996).

was borne by fleas carried in the hair of the black rat. It left scarcely a family intact.

Priests succumbed even as they ministered to the dying. "At night the death carts rattled through the alleys, and houses would yield up their dead if any of their inhabitants were well enough to drag out the corpses within." Great pits received the bodies. It was a time of unspeakable darkness, in which those who survived mourned not only the loss of these loved ones but also their possible damnation.[18]

We can only speculate on the details of Julian's early life. Her childhood, says Obbard, "would have been short as well as sombre," and she would have learned quickly the tasks essential to managing a household. A girl at the time would likely have been married at fifteen.

A second visit of the plague occurred in 1361, when Julian was nineteen. (It may well be, Obbard imagines, that by now she had married, and had been left without husband or child.) We do not know where, if at all, Julian received religious training or education. If her family were of means, she might have received rudimentary schooling at a convent. But from the looks of it, she had no such experience, and was rather only "a deeply religious young laywoman, touched early by death and sorrow."

---

[18] *Ibid.*, p. 10.

Early in her life Julian asked God for spiritual gifts that would enable her to understand His truth. At the age of thirty she found herself lying ill and near death. On the brink of leaving the world, she received a series of *shewings*, or revelations, that lasted for a period of two days. Julian, says Obbard, apparently did not have further visions in her lifetime. But in these hours she gained precious insight, it seems, into the mystery of Christ's death, the Trinity, and Mary the mother of God.

Julian recovered her health. But what might she do with her insight? In time, she retired to an anchorhold beside the church of St. Julian and St. Edward in Norwich and devoted the rest of her life to "pondering over what she had seen and heard in those packed hours when death was close." In *A Shewing of God's Love* she gave a brief account of her visions; about twenty years later, she composed a longer version. She became revered as a teacher and counselor, but her early life - her actual name, family and childhood experience - all passed into oblivion. She was known now simply as "the lady at St. Julian's," and in time as Julian.

The most famous words contained in this writing come in a passage in which Julian, describing the vision, recalls her perplexity at sin. How had sin come into existence?

Without it, she imagined, we all would have been pure and clean. Why had God, in His wisdom and foresight, not prevented it from coming into being? "I mourned and sorrowed over it," recalls Julian, "without reason and discretion." But Jesus, she explains, answered her by saying, "Sin is necessary, but all shall be well, and all shall be well, and all manner of thing shall be well."[19]

In this statement is the sum of all human destiny. If the words haunt us, perhaps it is because we sense their truth. This truth, of course, has no outward confirmation. We cannot see that Julian is correct. But we can feel that she is. Days pass, and scenes change. Comedy and tragedy have their time. Crises pass and recede into memory. Yet from all eternity comes assurance. With Julian's words we are beckoned Home with the promise that good will be wrought out of all present difficulty by a wisdom that surpasses our own.

---

[19] This passage from the *Shewings* is contained in a longer excerpt in Obbard, pp. 83-85. For Obbard's commentary on Julian as a writer and theologian, see pp. 35-43. See also text and commentary in Happold's volume.

IX

Intimations of Destiny

Human beings, it has been said, are amphibia; they live in two worlds at once, even if they are not wholly aware of it.[1] In the flights of mystics there are inklings of our own eternity; kindred elements may be present likewise in the common hard grain of daily life.

---

[1] Cf. again *The Cloud of Unknowing*: We need not strive in any outward direction for heaven, writes this author, "for we dwell there already through love and desire." (p. 126) Cited in this passage are the words of the apostle Paul, who says (*Philippians* 3: 20) that even now our life is in heaven.

Intimation in Childhood

Our birth is but a sleep and a forgetting;
The soul that rises with us, our life's star,
Hath had elsewhere its setting
And cometh from afar;
Not in entire forgetfulness,
And not in utter nakedness,
But trailing clouds of glory do we come
From God who is our home

William Wordsworth,
"Ode on Intimations of Immortality"

Where does it come from, this longing, this faint wish for something that we knew in our first years? Perhaps, writes J. B. Phillips, this wish for times past owes merely to the simplicity and relative ease of childhood. It may be that we are merely dulled, over time, by life's toil and imperfection, and have grown weary of the grind.

Or, he adds, this feeling may carry some deeper truth. It may be a kind of revelation. Perhaps it is not merely a longing, but "the eternal spirit in a man remembering here in his house of clay the shining joys of his real Home."[2]

---

[2] See relevant discussion in Phillips' earlier cited volume *Your God is Too Small*.

Our souls are awake in childhood, fresh and alive with a sense of magic. Unable now to relive the experience, we rely upon its faint echo. Yet we are not so far from Home. Wordsworth is by no means alone in this feeling, which ranges wide across human experience. One old Indian chief, in his final years, is said to have remarked that he enjoyed the company of small children, who were just coming from the place to which he was now returning. Tolstoy's Ivan Ilych, nearing his end, realizes that he has lost touch with truth as he has grown further from childhood. There, in his first years, "had been something really pleasant with which it would be possible to live if it could return."[3]

We as children, observes classicist and psychical researcher Frederic Myers, "did in a sense know much which we know no more."[4] Our picture of the universe then, how little complete, however erroneous, "wore some true colors." This faint stir, believes Myers, is not mere feeling, but real perception. A child, it is true, may yet lack the judgment of an adult. But if we are to discern the truth, we will have to recall these early impressions.

---

[3] Leo Tolstoy, *The Death of Ivan Ilych*. Trans. Aylmer Maude (New York: Signet Classic, 1960), p. 144.

[4] See Myers' "Greek Oracles", contained in his *Classical Essays* (London: Macmillan and Company, 1888).

The Weight of Glory

> In speaking of this desire ... I feel a certain shyness. I am almost committing an indecency. I am trying to rip open the inconsolable secret in each one of you - the secret which hurts so much that you take your revenge on it by calling it names like Nostalgia and Romanticism and Adolescence; the secret also which pierces with such sweetness that when, in very intimate conversation, the mention of it becomes imminent, we grow awkward and affect to laugh at ourselves; the secret we cannot hide and cannot tell, though we desire to do both.
>
> C. S. Lewis, "The Weight of Glory"

We may not confess it. But it is there, this deep yen for what is past the surrounding wall. We know that some truth answers. We know that somewhere the need is met.

Lewis addresses this subject in his essay "The Weight of Glory". He returns to it in a later book called *Surprised by Joy*. Life, he explains, has moments of desire with no natural object. In such moments we experience a joy that takes us beyond familiar categories of *happiness* or *pleasure*.[5]

---

[5] C. S. Lewis, *Surprised by Joy* (San Diego: Harcourt Brace and Company, 1955). See chapter 1, "The First Years".

The feeling, like these others, is desirable. Anyone who experiences it will want to experience it again. But here, says Lewis, the similarity ends. This joy is not within our power, while pleasure often is. Common ground aside, one might as well call this joy a kind of grief as to call it anything else. Yet in it we find something miraculous, something that will not quite let us go.

Lewis describes an early encounter with this experience, an occasion in his youth, when, standing by a flowering currant bush on a summer day, the sensation overtook him. It arose, he says, without warning, "as if from a depth not of years but of centuries." He was reminded of this feeling one morning, years later, when his brother brought into their nursery a miniature garden that he had constructed of tin, moss, twigs, and flowers.[6]

It is hard, says Lewis, to find the right words. A desire, of a certain kind - but for what? Before this could be known, "the desire itself was gone, the whole glimpse withdrawn, the world turned commonplace again, or only stirred by a longing for the longing that had just ceased." It had lasted but a moment, and still "in a certain sense everything else that had ever happened to me was insignificant in comparison."

---

[6] "As long as I live," writes Lewis, "my imagination of Paradise will retain something of my brother's toy garden." (p. 7)

We err, thinks Lewis, if we make this feeling an end in itself. Joy is not the goal of life. It is instead a consequence. Lewis' own mistake was to think that it is an object toward which effort must be directed. The real good, however, "lay in that of which Joy was the desiring."[7] In the end, joy itself proclaims, "You want - I myself am your want of - something other, outside, not you nor any state of you."

The question of what is this object, writes Lewis, brought him into the region of awe, into the realization that

> in deepest solitude there is a road right out of the self, a commerce with something which, by refusing to identify itself with any object of the senses, or anything whereof we have biological or social need, or anything imagined, or any state of our own minds, proclaims itself sheerly objective.[8]

Exploration of our own depths reveals an order of reality that exceeds the bounds of the visible world. In us is the intimation of a greater life and a higher destiny. We are beckoned toward a fulfillment surpassing any within present experience.

---

[7] *Ibid.*, p. 220.

[8] *Ibid.*, p. 221.

In the Best of Us a Presage

> The leaders of the race ... have always believed in immortality. They are not separated, in this case, from the masses of ignorant and superstitious men by doctrines of dissent. On the contrary, in this case, the ideas of the highest are at one with the hopes of the humblest of mankind.
>
> John Haynes Holmes,
> "Ten Reasons for Believing in Immortality"

There have long been reasons advanced to show that the soul must perish with the body. But so are there arguments for our survival. It is significant, says John Haynes Holmes, that so many of our greatest personalities have believed in a future life.[9]

Those who have been intrigued by the idea, says Holmes, include philosophers, such as Plato, Kant, and Henri Bergson; scientists like Charles Darwin and Arthur Eddington; and inspirers of men like Socrates, Tolstoy, and Mahatma Gandhi. Even heretics like Voltaire and Thomas Paine "stand in awe before this conception of eternity."

---

[9] Holmes' "Ten Reasons for Believing in Immortality" is contained in Paul Edwards and Arthur Pap, eds., *A Modern Introduction to Philosophy* (New York: Macmillan, 1973). This part of Holmes discussion can be found on pp. 253-54.

The popularity of a belief, of course, does not prove its worth. But where immortality is concerned, there exists a noteworthy connection between the belief and the personality in which it appears. It is so often the greatest of us, the highest examples, the ones most strongly infused with the truth, who believe in survival.

Let us imagine, for a moment, that this belief is false. In that case, who are the ones in error? They are not, as James Martineau explains, "the mean and grovelling souls who never reached to so great a thought." Instead they are "the great and holy, whom all men revere," the ones "who have lived for something better than their happiness and spent themselves on the altar of human good."

Granted, truth and decency may be at odds in the final analysis. But if so, Holmes observes, we have a very curious situation. For then the same constitution that makes for greatness, as we normally reckon it, makes us fools in reality.

Holmes' point might be put in terms of a question. What do we really think of a Buddha, a William Blake, or an Aurobindo? If the other world is not real, then where lies their wisdom? Perhaps rather than sages or seers we ought to count them as being defectives - perhaps even as idiots or lunatics.

Skeptics, of course, can still deny the reality of survival. The mystic and otherworldly types just noted, they may say, are sincere and pleasant folk, but they are nonetheless mistaken. Such a view does not seem, on the face of it, to contain any breach of logic. But is it the better alternative?[10]

Whom ought we to hold in esteem, and what are we to believe, if the inspirations of the highest among us are but illusions? When we see a Mother Teresa devote her long life to service in dens of misery, what is our verdict?

Our usual reaction, it seems, is one of respect, even awe. But why this, unless we recognize, at some level, an order of reality in which material standards are overturned on a higher scale? When we see compassion, otherworldliness, genuine self-sacrifice, we seem to be unable to say such a thing. Perhaps the reason is that in some part of ourselves we know better.

---

[10] Indeed I must wonder how often skeptics themselves stand by their view when it comes to practical life-choices. Catch one of them in a serious moment, and he or she, too, will likely betray a respect for the saint and the moralist. These deniers have no use, they say, for the unseen, for what they cannot weigh and touch; they have no use, then, for "higher" values and visions. Yet watch them in times of hardship or crisis. They will abide by a sense of duty, in many cases, against odds and at the expense of all worldly advantage. To what end, if this world is the only measure?

Body and Soul

> ... our souls have potentialities and promises which should not, as indeed they cannot, be subject to the chance vicissitudes of earthly fortune.
>
> John Haynes Holmes,
> "Ten Reasons for Believing in Immortality"

If we would have insight into eternity, believes Holmes, we might look into ourselves. In so doing we will discover "a lack of coordination" between our personalities and the material world in which they develop. Our souls have qualities that resist assimilation to the categories of material happenstance. Their "potentialities and promises" cannot obey the shifting sands of earthly fortune.[11]

What should we say when we see some life of nobility and elevation cut off abruptly by stray events of the moment? Holmes cites the example of Shelley, drowned in his thirtieth year by a heedless sea, of the explorer Captain Scott "frozen in mid-career" by a chance event of weather. Is it possible that these lives of ours are dependent upon "a fall of snow, a grain of dust, a passing breeze"?

---

[11] "Ten Reasons for Believing in Immortality", p. 256.

Ought we to think that eternal powers are annihilated by transient accidents? Says Holmes, "I cannot think so!" For the greatness of human beings provides us with an insight into their destiny. In courage, in noble aspiration, lies something that transcends material fact.

The practical worth of belief in immortality, may furnish another and corroborating index. Whatever is true "enlarges and lifts and strengthens the life of man," while what is false does the opposite. Truth, it seems, conduces to life, as nourishment conduces to health. What is the impact of belief in survival upon the life that we now live?

A believer lives in a universe "where spiritual, not material forces, prevail"; it is one wherein personality, in ourselves and in others, is precious, and ought to be conserved. It is a world in which principles, not possessions, are the supreme concern of life; where labors are not in vain, and sacrifice is not foolish, where love is the greatest thing in the world. The individual who lives life in such terms, says Holmes, takes on immortal qualities: "His character assumes the proportions of his faith, and his work the range of his high destiny." He quotes Harry Emerson Fosdick, who says that belief in immortality makes for great living. Therefore, writes Holmes, "I believe in immortality."

Revelation in Daily Encounter

> And love, above all when it struggles against destiny, overwhelms us with the feeling of the vanity of this world of appearances and gives us a glimpse of another world, in which destiny is overcome and liberty is law.
>
> Miguel de Unamuno, *The Tragic Sense of Life*

Life, writes Unamuno, holds no greater concern than personal immortality. Once awakening to the prospect, we cannot think otherwise. Eternity is the first question, the one from which all others gain importance.

But while the soul demands immortality, says Unamuno, the intellect denies it. We cannot have rational confidence in our own survival, indeed reason tends to push us in the other direction. From this collision is born what he calls *the tragic sense of life*. It is an unrelenting warfare of head and heart that finds no logical resolution.

What is our response? The solution to this problem, he contends, is not found in theoretical "proofs" of the kind that abound in the history of philosophy. Any such proof is but sleight-of-hand, the product that issues from the author's own prior conviction. Such theses, however good their argument, are the expression of a deeper will.

If we are to live in good faith, we must instead face the challenge head-on, knowing that our deepest need will not find intellectual satisfaction. Out of this act of courage, believes Unamuno, will develop an understanding. In love, we find the basis for faith.

Survival, by the gauge of the intellect, is unlikely. Yet we must believe. At the bottom of this abyss, we are thus left with reason and vital feeling, neither of which can surrender to the other.

There is, thinks Unamuno, something intensifying in this life. In our union with others is revelation, truth that is felt as much as reasoned. Never is love more revealing than when it must contend with those "diamond-hard laws of destiny" that deny its full expression. The more that this world refuses us, the more it kindles our sense of eternity. Lovers in this condition, writes Unamuno,

> establish their love beyond the confines of the world, and the strength of this poor love suffering beneath the yoke of Destiny gives them intuition of another world where there is no other law than the liberty of love - another world where there are no barriers because there is no flesh.[12]

---

[12] Miguel de Unamuno, *The Tragic Sense of Life*. Trans. J. Crawford Flitch (New York: Dover Publications, Inc., 1954), p. 136.

A Life Redeemed

"Death is finished," he said to himself. "It is no more!"

Leo Tolstoy, *The Death of Ivan Ilych*

For most of us, death has a convenient place, locked away and kept at a distance. But one day it may come through the door without warning and take us by surprise. Tolstoy describes such a case in his novel *The Death of Ivan Ilych*. It is the story of a man who passes his life in routine fashion and one day finds that he is dying. Ivan, like Tolstoy,[13] is a man of success who climbs the social ladder. He builds a career in civil service, presiding in time over court cases and keeping appearances on every front.

The story begins with news of Ivan's passing, and with the a notice announcing his wife's "profound sorrow" over her husband's demise. Ivan's colleagues attend the service, observing rules of etiquette while each nursing some secret ambition. Present everywhere is an unspoken sense of relief at the fact that "it is he who is dead and not I."

---

[13] See Tolstoy's autobiographical *A Confession*. Trans. Aylmer Maude (London: Oxford University Press, 1974), contained in one volume with Tolstoy's *The Gospel in Brief* and *What I Believe*.

What has led to this day? Ivan, it is explained, has lived a good life by outward measure. He has earned position among his colleagues. His marriage, to appearances, is solid. His home is well furnished. But something in his life is missing.

One day Ivan is inside his house, on a ladder, adding decoration to a window. He slips and suffers a seemingly minor accident, hitting his side on the knob of a window frame in the effort to maintain his balance. It does not seem like much at first, and little is thought of it. But weeks pass and the pain increases.

As his condition worsens, Ivan grows worried, and then desperate. To his horror, he now finds himself looked upon by others with the same habitual indifference that he has shown them. For Ivan has always sought to minimize involvement and to insure his own convenience .

Ivan sees that he is dying. He looks back upon his life and realizes that it has been empty. The further from childhood, it seems, the less genuine his existence. Ivan's life, explains Tolstoy, has been "most simple and most ordinary and therefore most terrible."[14] Ivan himself now sees this. Yet how can it be, he asks at last, "when I did everything properly?"[15]

---

[14] *Ivan Ilych*, p. 102.

[15] *Ibid.*, p. 145.

How, indeed? Ivan, it seems, has never been true to himself. He has passed his time by conforming to station, by valuing and enjoying what others seem to value and enjoy. There is a sense, thinks Tolstoy, in which he has never grasped his own mortality. The syllogism in his logic text, "Caius is a man, men are mortal, therefore Caius is mortal," has seemed right to him - as applied to Caius. He, on the other hand, "had been little Vanya, with a mamma and a papa, with Mitya and Volodya, with the toys, a coachman and a nurse, afterwards with Katenka and with all the joys, griefs, and delights of childhood, boyhood, and youth." What did Caius know of the scents, the silken touches, the young riots and flooding emotions of a real life? Ivan was not Caius.

Ivan's life is absurd. But is it unusual? To live in this self-preoccupied fashion, never to ask what is truly important, is tragic. Yet perhaps we and Ivan have common ground. It would be easier if Tolstoy's protagonist were some villain, some freak or aberration we might put at a distance. But instead, we hear, he has lived a life terrible and *ordinary*. Might his life be ours?

A lesser author might have let Ivan die and been done with it. But there is more. A greater truth dawns in Ivan's final days. He comes to know something of life that he has not known before.

Two hours before his death he feels his young son at his bedside, kissing his hand and shedding tears. At that moment, writes Tolstoy, "Ivan Ilych fell through and caught sight of the light, and it was revealed to him that though his life had not been what it should have been, this could still be rectified."[16] Ivan says that he is sorry. He asks forgiveness.

At this same moment, he seeks his own fear of death and does not find it. There is no longer any fear, because there is no death. "In place of death there was light." For those present, the process of Ivan's death continues for two hours. "It is finished," says one at last. Ivan hears these words and repeats them in his soul. "Death is finished," he says to himself. "It is no more!"

---

[16] *Ibid.*, p. 151.

Nostalgia is essentially forward-looking.

X

The Life Ahead

Much in this book expresses the anticipation of a greater life awaiting. Our encounter with value, our deep connection with other people - certain elements of present experience encourage a view of life that extends beyond earthly bounds. If indeed another life awaits, what sort of life might it be?

One finds no shortage of ideas. Now and again, it seems, is an actual glimpse across the divide: An influence is felt from a place unseen; a door opens in life's final moments and light from the other side enters; someone "returns," claiming to have gone over and returned.

There are some who find a basis for belief in the speech or writing of alleged "mediums." Others, as we have seen, find cause for hope in the substance of ordinary life. In each case, perhaps, we find some hint of what lies past the gate. This chapter explores the issue further.

Purported Glimpses

> She died at half-past six o'clock on the evening of Saturday, June 8th. She had roused and bidden her friends good-bye, and was talking of dying, and seemed to have no fear. She appeared to see one and another of the friends she knew were dead. So far it was like other similar cases. But now suddenly, and with every appearance of surprise, she turned to her father and exclaimed, "Why, papa, I am going to take Jennie with me!" Then she added, "Why, papa! You did not tell me Jennie was here!" And immediately she reached out her arms as if in welcome, and said, "Oh, Jennie, I'm so glad you are here!"
>
> Sir William Barrett, *Death-Bed Visions*

In 1976 a philosophy teacher and medical doctor named Ray Moody caused a stir with his book *Life After Life*. It describes the experiences of those near death who have "crossed over" and returned to tell the story.

These near-death experiences, says Moody, share many common features; they also resemble experiences recounted in classic sources like Plato's *Republic*, the Tibetan *Book of the Dead*, and the New Testament.[1]

---

[1] See again Moody's *Life After Life*, especially chapter 3.

Moody's book was preceded by fifty years by a kindred work called *Death-Bed Visions*.[2] Its posthumous author was Sir William Barrett. Years earlier, a young professor of physics in Ireland, Barrett had developed an interest in the paranormal. He helped to found the Society for Psychical Research with Cambridge classicist Frederic Myers and Professor Henry Sidgwick in 1882.[3]

The Society sought to apply methods of systematic investigation to various examples of these phenomena. Among its concerns were thought-transference, clairvoyance, and seance mediumship. *Death-Bed Visions* draws material from cases of Barrett's own acquaintance. It describes the visions of dying individuals who seem to catch sight of another world as they are leaving this one. In some cases this vision seems to convey knowledge that cannot be explained by ordinary means. Thus a small child, for example, may claim to see a friend or relative on the other side about whose death the child has never been told. There are also cases in which extraordinary sights and sounds are witnessed by those in attendance.[4]

---

[2] Sir William Barrett, *Death-Bed Visions* (Northamptonshire, England: Aquarian Press, 1986).

[3] See introductory comment by series editor Colin Wilson.

[4] See chapter 2, "Visions Seen by the Dying of Persons Unknown by them to be Dead". Cases of sights and sounds perceived by those in attendance are noted in the last two chapters.

Some explain near-death experiences in terms of events deep within the psyche or nervous system. Yet many of Barrett's examples are hard to explain in this fashion. How, for example, can a defense mechanism, or a failing brain circuitry, explain cases like these just noted? The experience is also quite distinct, it seems, from those episodes produced by mind-altering drugs.

At times, the force of the experience may carry over to those in attendance. Barrett cites the case reported by Dr. Williams, present at the death of well-known American tenor singer James Moore. In his last moments, Moore took Williams' hand and thanked him for his care. Then Moore began to speak to his own departed mother, whom he saw waiting as if across a boundary. "On his face," recalls Williams, "there was a look of inexpressible happiness, and the way in which he said the words impressed me as I have never been before, and I am as firmly convinced that he saw and talked with his mother as I am that I am sitting here."[5]

---

[5] *Ibid.*, pp. 54-55.

Sound and Light

> There is water in abundance in the rivers and streams and brooks, and every drop of it not only fit to drink, but, indeed, like no water to be found upon earth. It glistens and sparkles; it is crystal clear; it is buoyant; one can slip beneath its surface and enjoy its warm embrace as it folds its living arms about you.
>
> Anthony Borgia, *Here and Hereafter*

This statement comes from a book written several decades ago.[6] It purports to be an eyewitness account of the next world produced by communication through a medium by "automatic writing."

The water, we are told, "was as clear as crystal, and the light was reflected back in every ripple and tiny wave in almost dazzlingly bright colors. It was unbelievably soft to the touch, and its buoyancy ... supported whatever was in it." Warmth, fragrance, nectar; a pervading comfort - everywhere is joy and light.

---

[6] Anthony Borgia, *Life in the World Unseen* (Midway, Utah: M. A. P., Inc., 1993). This book, which had its first printing more than forty years ago, purports to be a communication through the hand of Borgia from the departed Robert Hugh Benson, earthly son of Edward White Benson, a former archbishop of Canterbury.

This account, delivered by Anthony Borgia, speaks constantly of brightness and fulfillment. Much is said of sound and color, and their relation. Color and musical tone are "interchangeable," one giving rise to the other.

> In the spirit world all music is color, and all color is music. The one is never existent without the other. That is why the flowers give forth such pleasant tones when they are approached ... The water that sparkles and flashes colors is also creating sounds of musical purity ....[7]

It is a pleasant account. Such accounts have been around for awhile, and some are quite engaging. It is a separate question, of course, what credence they deserve. Borgia's account will strike some as being fanciful, as being perhaps also too "physical" in its description. It reads too much, they may say, as a glorified version of life in this world.

Yet descriptions like this one merit attention, I think, if only for their capacity to stir the imagination. They require us to examine our own ideas. Many of us entertain the possibility of a future life. Some of us even believe that such a life awaits. "Heaven," we call it; our "just reward," we imagine. But what does this mean? How might we envision the next stage of our destiny?

---

[7] *Ibid.*, p. 70.

Perhaps the next world bears some resemblance to this one. We describe certain features of our present experience - those present, for example, in certain instances of nature, of fine art, of human emotion - as being "ethereal" and "otherworldly." We say that they elevate us, that they reveal to us some insight into the higher nature of things.[8] If we hold true to our instincts, we might view these features as furnishing some presage of our destiny. In which case, we might suppose, the description just cited is not so far off the mark.

Borgia's remarks about sound and color are indeed unusual. But they have, it might be remarked, a curious parallel in sources within the historical religious mainstream. Evelyn Underhill, whose work we have noted, quotes St. Martin as saying, "I saw flowers that sounded, and saw notes that shone." Certain mystics, she explains, have moments "in which the senses are fused into a single and ineffable act of perception, and color and sound are known as aspects of one thing."[9]

---

[8] Pressed for an example in music, I would cite the Pachelbel *Canon* as one of many.

[9] Evelyn Hill, *Mysticism* (New York: New American Library, 1974), p. 7. This book had its first printing in 1911.

The Reality of Justice

> I condole with you. We have lost a most dear and valuable relation. *But it is the will of God and nature that these mortal bodies be laid aside when the soul is to enter into real life.* This is rather an embryo state, a preparation for living. A man is not completely born until he is dead. When then should we grieve that a new child is born among the immortals, a new member added to their happy society?
>
> Benjamin Franklin,
> personal correspondence

Often we hear cited the political wisdom of those individuals who were instrumental in the founding of our nation. Brilliant and great-souled men, they were possessed, it seems, by an innate love of liberty and justice. Our own freedom in this day owes much to their conviction.

We find in them a source of religious wisdom, as well. They were men, in some cases, with a strong prevision of the next life. Unconsumed by doctrinal issues, they were open-ended believers in the reality of providence and the survival of the human spirit. They were likewise believers in an ultimate justice.

We will be judged, said Thomas Jefferson, not so much by the particular rightness of our beliefs as by their *uprightness*.[10] One could search many volumes for a more succinct wisdom.

The personal correspondences of Benjamin Franklin reveal this same conviction. Reflecting upon that man who commits atrocity in this world, Franklin remarks,

> and yet this man lives, enjoys all the good things this world can afford, and is surrounded by flatterers, who keep even his conscience quiet by telling him he is the best of princes! *I wonder at this, but I cannot therefore part with the comfortable belief of a Divine Providence; and the more I see the impossibility, from the number and extent of his crimes, of giving equivalent punishment to a wicked man in this life, the more I am convinced of a future state, in which all that here appears to be wrong shall be set right, all that is crooked made straight*.[11]

Belief in the hereafter is sometimes dismissed as being the product of wish-fulfillment. We want, it is said,

---

[10] This remark is contained in a letter to his nephew Peter Carr. Our reason, says Jefferson, is the oracle that is given to us by heaven. See the letter of August 10th, 1787 contained in *The Portable Thomas Jefferson*. Ed. Merrill D. Peterson (New York: Penguin Books, 1975), pp. 423-28.

[11] This quotation is contained in George L. Rogers' annotated edition of Franklin's *The Art of Virtue* (Eden Prairie, Minnesota: Acorn Publishing, 1996). The particular occasion for Franklin's statement was an unprovoked massacre of the Moravian Indians.

a softer, more pleasant existence, and so we fashion another world to compensate for this one. But Franklin's words express more than this. Near the end of his own life, he writes to a friend,

> I often think on the happy days I passed in England with my and your learned and ingenious friends, who have left us to join the majority in the world of spirits. Every one of them now knows more than all of us they have left behind. *It is to me a comfortable reflection, that, since we must live forever in a future state, there is a sufficient stock of amusement in reserve for us, to be found in constantly learning something new to eternity, the present quantity of human ignorance infinitely exceeding that of human knowledge*. Adieu, my dear friend, and believe me, in whatever world, yours most affectionately.[12]

If one reads these words carefully, one sees that they express not merely desire, but ambition. In eternity, believes Franklin, is the prospect not merely of self-indulgence but of self-improvement. Seeing that nothing is ever truly annihilated, he writes to another acquaintance, "I believe I shall, in some shape or other, always exist; and, with all the inconveniences human life is liable to, I shall not exist to a new edition of mine; hoping, however, that the *errata* of the last may be corrected."

---

[12] *Ibid.*, p. 87.

Higher Worlds and Moral Gravitation

> We see only material things, and they are not ultimately satisfying; we feel that we are dwellers in an unseen reality of which we catch only occasional glimpses.
>
> Oliver Lodge, *Phantom Walls*

Franklin's expectation of justice is not unique. It finds agreement in many places, including literature associated with the Society for Psychical Research.

Oliver Lodge was a renowned physicist and Society member who wrote a number of books concerning science and religion. Our exploration of the material universe, he maintained, is no obstacle to belief in realities beyond. Principles of science, he held, might even be applied to investigation of this outlying region. Lodge cites the example of seance mediumship, where on occasion factual material is produced for which there seems to be no natural explanation.[13]

---

[13] Thus the controls (i. e., seeming otherworld communicators) at times gave every evidence of being the departed individuals with whom contact was sought. See Oliver Lodge, *The Survival of Man* (London: Methuen and Co., Ltd., 1911), especially Section IV, "Automatism and Lucidity". For an excellent history, see Alfred Douglas, *E S P - A Century of Psychical Research* (Woodstock, New York: Overlook Press, 1977). See also Alan Gauld, *Mediumship and Survival* (London: Paladin, 1982).

The consensus of this purported communication, says Lodge, is that the next world is really a series of places fitted to individual development. There is said to be "plenty of room," so that each of us may find appropriate residence. We take with us, it seems, the effects of actions that we have chosen in this world. Thus while happiness may be more abundant on that side, we are not "suddenly transmuted" into wholly new beings on our arrival.[14] There is likewise "a sorting-out process": We cannot enter into company for which we are not ready, and we are not disturbed by those unworthy of our own.

This theme of gradation is present across the world's religious traditions. We have noted, for one, the tradition of India.[15] At its heart is a sense of reciprocity, of final balance, where human action is concerned. Here one finds *karma*, a law that is to the moral sphere what action and reaction are to the world of classical physics. By its rule we reap what we sow, in the long run, with every action. Our progress, on this view, can take whole lifetimes.[16]

---

[14] *Ibid.*, p. 233.

[15] See again discussion in chapters 3 and 8.

[16] The traditional Sanskrit conception, again, is that of *moksha*, freedom and release from the limitations of earthly existence. A related idea, prominent in Buddhist tradition, is that of *nirvana*, literally a blowing out, or extinguishing, as of a flame. This term conveys, it seems, the extinguishing of egoistic desires that perpetuate the wheel of rebirth.

No effort is insignificant. Each has its influence. "If I chop down a tree that blocks my view," writes Huston Smith,[17] "each stroke of the ax unsettles the tree; but it leaves its mark on me as well, driving deeper into my being my determination to have my way in the world." All that I do for selfish reasons "adds another layer to my ego," which insulates me from the truth. By the same token, "every act done without thought for myself diminishes my self-centeredness until finally no barrier remains to separate me from the divine."[18]

Thus no constructive action, it seems, is ever lost. An expression of this idea occurs in the earlier-noted *Bhagavad-Gita*, where the warrior Arjuna must persevere in his caste-duty to win liberation. Despairing, Arjuna asks what happens to those who try, but fall short of this goal.

"When a man goes astray from the path to Brahman," he says, "he has missed both lives, the worldly and the spiritual. He has no support anywhere. Is he not

---

[17] Huston Smith, *The World's Religions* (San Francisco, HarperCollins, 1991), p. 38. This observation is made in Smith's discussions of the four principal forms of *yoga*, the "yoking" or "union" of oneself to the divine. These forms are fitted respectively to different personality types, thus one emphasizing *jnana*, or abstract knowledge, another *bhakti*, or personal devotion, and a third *raja*, or intensified meditation.

[18] *Ibid.* See related discussion in chapter 5 of Eliot Deutsch, *Advaita Vedanta: A Philosophical Reconstruction* (Honolulu: The University Press of Hawaii, 1980).

lost, as a broken cloud is lost in the sky?"[19] Krishna replies that this one is not lost, "either in this world or the next. For no one who seeks Brahman ever comes to an evil end." Such an individual wins "the heaven of the doers of good deeds, and dwell there many long years." This one will enjoy the fruits of his effort before eventually being returned to finish the task, now closer to the end for his striving.

---

[19] See chapter 6, verses 37 and 38 (Prabhavananda translation).

How are We Viewed from the Other Side?

> So it seems to me that those who have found out to a certainty what the grand issue of life means, cannot be troubled because we shed a few tears over a loss in Wall Street or because we have a pain which may last us for a week. They know what is before us, they know it is to be victory in time; and perhaps they know that these experiences of suffering that we are passing through, are part of the training that is to make us capable of entering into the joy and felicity which they have found their own.
>
> Minot Savage, *Life Beyond Death*

A question arises concerning the situation of those who have left this world. Often we hear that they are able to see us from the other side. But if so, it seems, such knowledge may weigh them down. For they cannot be very happy when they see us still struggling here against the challenges of daily life.

This question is addressed by Minot Savage, a philosopher and another early member of the Society for Psychical Research. Those on the other side, says Savage, may indeed be witness to our difficulties. But this need not mean that they are burdened by the sight. For they may not in the earthly estimate of the problem.

Consider, says Savage, the mother with her child playing at her feet. The child breaks a plaything. It is "heart-breaking sorrow to the little one," observes Savage, yet it need not affect the mother in this way. She picks up the child and comforts her, knowing that this crisis will not last.

In similar fashion, those on the other side may realize that our present difficulties are not the absolute concerns that we imagine. They perceive our situation in the light of eternity. They see likewise the nearness of our return. The real question, they realize, is not our present circumstance, but the quality of the spirit that is forged out of it. Our difficulties may indeed look very different from above. By adopting this point of view, from time to time, we ourselves might gain perspective.

An Adventure into Eternity

> In the midst of this present 'fallen' or illusion-bound existence, in which the human fragments look at each other through the slits of separate ego-masks, the sense of our ultimate belonging together in total community is the unselfish love which the New Testament calls *agape* ... What Christians call the Mystical Body of Christ within the life of God, and Hindus the universal Atman which we all are, and mahayana Buddhists the self-transcending unity in the Dharma Body of the Buddha, consists of the wholeness of ultimately perfected humanity beyond the existence of separate egos.
>
> John Hick, *Death and Eternal Life*

We often imagine that the world's great religions are in conflict, that they compete, much like rival leaders, for our own allegiance. To accept one, we may imagine, is to forsake all the others.

Yet might it be otherwise? Might these faiths share some basic truth? Their traditions, writes John Hick, are historically different, but at a deeper level they may find agreement. Their true message may point us in a common direction.

Hick's *Death and Eternal Life* traces a possible account of our progress from this world to the next.[20] Its task, he explains, is global theology, investigation that speaks plausibly to the human religious experience across time and culture. To this end it incorporates material from literature of wide array.

Our religious sensibility, says Hick, finds expression in our notion of *the soul*, of a self-conscious entity possessed of an unconditional worth. Selfhood, by the same token, has two "polar aspects," which Hick calls the *ego* and the *person*. The first is an "enclosed" entity that excludes and is excluded by others like itself. It seeks to preserve in its encounters an "egocentric poise." As such it lives in that condition of *angst* and estrangement that has various cultural expressions.[21]

The second and higher of these aspects is our personal nature. It is essentially inter-personal and develops through our involvement with other centers of consciousness like ourselves. It is, says Hick, an integral part "of the totality of interpersonal life." While self as ego is "solitary and protective," the person is open. It is "inherently self-giving" and able to exist in community.

---

[20] John Hick, *Death and Eternal Life* (Louisville, Kentucky: Westminster / John Knox Press, 1994).

[21] See pp. 49 and following in chapter 2, "What is Man?".

The common western idea of a single life in this world followed by an endless existence in a single place, thinks Hick, makes little sense, and its moral scheme is incoherent. The strand of Eastern belief that envisions countless returns to this world, he maintains, is no better. The popular notion of rebirth might instead be viewed as a mythological expression of a real progress involving separate life-adventures over the course of our development. We might see this as a "vertical" progress into higher worlds, rather than an endless recycling in this one.[22]

The world's major religious traditions, observes Hick, speak characteristically not only of progress, but of liberation. This event is commonly envisioned as being, in some sense, a *unitive* state, a merging of oneself with an ultimate reality. The nature of this unification is a longstanding mystery, but perhaps we have some intimation in our present experience. Our insight into the nature of personality may provide a clue.

Throughout a good part of Western history, the self has been looked upon as being something wholly and substantially distinct from its fellows. But there has since come emphasis upon its interpersonal nature.

---

[22] For a detailed discussion for the rationale of this view, see section 5, "A Possible Human Destiny".

"Could it be," asks Hick, "that as the separate ego-selves attain their several human perfections the boundaries between them become more transparent and human existence becomes more corporate than individual?"

This distinction between ego and person suggests that as an individual becomes more developed, he or she becomes less an ego. The developed personality is essentially outward-looking and unbound by selfish limit. This progress may offer us direction concerning our greater development.

Perhaps, says Hick, a wholly developed individual is a self without egoity, "a living consciousness which is transparent to the other consciousnesses in relation to which it lives in a full community of love."[23] Thus it may be that in progressively higher worlds,

> the interpersonality of mutual love becomes the universal principle of life, whilst self-protective egoity withers away, so that the individual's series of lives culminates in a last life beyond which there is no further embodiment but instead entry into the common Vision of God, or nirvana, or the eternal consciousness of the atman in its relation to Ultimate Reality.[24]

---

[23] *Ibid.*, p. 460.

[24] *Ibid.*, p. 464.

Land in Sight

> What lies across the sea he cannot tell; his special expectations all may be mistaken; but his insight into the clear meaning of present facts may persuade him beyond doubt that the sea has another shore.
>
> H. E. Fosdick, *The Assurance of Immortality*

We cannot yet see all that awaits. We have not set foot on the shore. This moment finds us on the sea, land but dim through the mist. Yet within us even now is a sense of direction. The ship is headed Home.

Deep within lies assurance. In daily life we find its ground. Our wish for days past, as we have seen, provides one occasion. It is, say some, is a desire to return to the past. But if we were to return, C. S. Lewis has said, this desired moment would only refer us back to something else again.[25]

In order to understand this feeling, we must look not back, but ahead. In it we find not mere want but an element of the sacred. In it we sound our own depths. The real object of our desire is not past; rather it is timeless. Nostalgia is essentially forward-looking.

---

[25] See again discussion in his *Surprised by Joy*.

In our relations, in our shared moments with others, we find our real destiny. Moments of shared laughter, of burden, of hope and assurance, reveal to us that our greatest desires are destined not for want, but for realization. Given to us in those moments is not proof, but occasion. In them is the voice of eternity.

Bibliography

Mortimer Adler, *Six Great Ideas* (New York: Macmillan Books, 1981).

St. Augustine, *The City of God*. Trans. John Healey (London: J. M. Dent and Sons Ltd., 1947). Two volumes.

A. J. Ayer, *Language, Truth and Logic* (New York: Dover Books, 1952).

William Barrett, *Irrational Man* (New York: Doubleday Books, 1990).

Sir William Barrett, *Death-Bed Visions* (Northamptonshire, England: Aquarian Press, 1986).

Robert Barron, *Thomas Aquinas - Spiritual Master* (New York: Crossroad Publishing Co., 1996).

Anthony Borgia, *Life in the World Unseen* (Midway, Utah: M. A. P., Inc. 1993).

Eugene Borowitz, *A Layman's Introduction to Religious Existentialism* (Philadelphia: Westminster Press, 1965).

Dale Carnegie, *How to Make Friends and Influence People* (New York: Simon and Schuster, 1982).

Gale E. Christianson, *In the Presence of the Creator - Isaac Newton and His Times* (New York: Free Press, 1984).

Roy J. Cook, ed., *One Hundred and One Famous Poems* (Chicago: Contemporary Books, 1958).

Eliot Deutsch, *Advaita Vedanta - A Philosophical Reconstruction* (Honolulu: The University Press of Hawaii, 1980).

Fyodor Dostoevsky, *The Brothers Karamazov*. Trans. Constance Garnett (New York: The Modern Library, 1950).

Alfred Douglas, *Extra Sensory Powers - A Century of Psychical Research* (Woodstock, New York: Overlook Press, 1977).

Terry Eagleton, *The Ideology of the Aesthetic* (Oxford: Basil Blackwell, 1990).

Paul Edwards and Arthur Pap, eds., *A Modern Introduction to Philosophy* (New York: Macmillan, 1973).

Epictetus, *The Art of Living*. Trans. Sharon Lebell (San Francisco: HarperCollins, 1995).

Harry Emerson Fosdick, *On Being a Real Person* (New York: Harper and Brothers Publishers, 1943).

Viktor Frankl, *Man's Search for Meaning* (New York: Washington Square Press, 1984).

_______, *Psychoanalysis and Existentialism* (New York: Simon and Schuster, 1967).

_______, *The Will to Meaning* (New York: NAL Dutton, 1988).

Benjamin Franklin, *The Art of Virtue*. Ed. George L. Rogers (Eden Prairie, Minnesota: 1996).

Carl J. Friedrich, ed., *The Philosophy of Kant* (New York: Modern Library, 1993).

Alan Gauld, *Mediumship and Survival* (London: Paladin Books, 1982).

Georg Gadamer, *The Relevance of the Beautiful and other essays* (Cambridge: Cambridge University Press, 1986).

W. K. C. Guthrie, *The Sophists* (Cambridge: Cambridge University Press, 1971).

Elizabeth Hamilton and Huntington Cairns, eds., *The Collected Dialogues of Plato* (Princeton, New Jersey: Princeton University Press, 1973).

F. C. Happold, ed., *Mysticism - A Study and An Anthology* (London: Penguin Books, 1988).

G. B. Harrison, ed., *A Book of English Poetry* (London: Penguin Books, 1950).

Andrew Harvey, ed., *The Essential Mystics* (San Francisco: HarperCollins, 1997).

John O. Hayden, ed., *William Wordsworth: Selected Poems* (London: Penguin Books, 1994).

Hesiod, *Theogony* and *Works and Days*. Trans. M. L. West (Oxford: Oxford University Press, 1988).

Eugen Herrigel, *Zen in the Art of Archery* (New York: Vintage Books, 1989).

John Hick, *Evil and the God of Love* (New York: Harper and Row, 1966).

_______, *Death and Eternal Life* (Louisville: Westminster / John Knox Press, 1994).

The Holy Bible Containing the Old and New Testaments (New York: Thomas Nelson and Sons, 1901). American Standard Version.

William James, *The Varieties of Religious Experience* (New York: Macmillan Books, 1961).

_______, *The Will to Believe and other essays* and *Human Immortality* (New York: Dover Books, 1956).

William Johnston, ed., *The Cloud of Unknowing* (New York: Image Books, 1996).

W. T. Jones, *A History of Western Philosophy* (Ft. Worth, Texas: Harcourt Brace Jovanovich College Publishers, 1980). Five volumes.

Immanuel Kant, *Critique of Practical Reason*. Trans. Lewis White Beck (New York: Liberal Arts Press, 1956).

_______, *Observations on the Feeling of the Beautiful and Sublime*. Trans. John T. Goldthwait (Berkeley: University of California Press, 1960).

Walter Kaufmann, *The Faith of a Heretic* (New York: Doubleday and Co., 1961).

Soren Kierkegaard, *Concluding Unscientific Postscript*. Trans. David L. Swenson and Walter Lowrie (Princeton, New Jersey: Princeton University Press, 1944).

G. S. Kirk and J. E. Raven, eds., *The Presocratic Philosophers* (Cambridge: Cambridge University Press, 1969).

Robert Leckie, *George Washington's War - the Saga of the American Revolution* (New York: HarperCollins, 1992).

C. S. Lewis, *The Abolition of Man* (New York: Simon and Schuster, 1996).

________, *Surprised by Joy* (San Diego: Harcourt and Company, 1955).

________, *The Weight of Glory and other addresses* (New York: Collier Books, 1980).

Sir Oliver Lodge, *Phantom Walls* (New York: G. P. Putnam's Sons, 1930).

________, *The Survival of Man* (London: Methuen and Company Ltd., 1911).

Mickey Mantle, *The Mick* (New York: Jove Books, 1985).

J. S. Mill, *On Liberty* (New York: Liberal Arts Press, 1956).

E. L. Miller, *God and Reason* (Englewood Cliffs, New Jersey: Prentice-Hall, 1995).

Raymond Moody, Jr., *Life After Life* (New York: Bantam Books, 1975).

F. W. H. Myers, *Essays - Classical* (London: Macmillan and Company, 1888).

Elizabeth Ruth Obbard, *Introducing Julian - Woman of Norwich* (Hyde Park, New York: New City Press, 1996).

The Upanishads. Trans. Swami Nikhilananda (New York: Ramakrishna-Vivekananda Center, 1949). Four volumes.

Norman Vincent Peale, *The Power of Positive Thinking* (New York: Fawcett Crest, 1992).

J. B. Phillips, *Your God is Too Small* (New York: Collier Books, 1961).

Merrill D. Peterson, ed., *The Portable Thomas Jefferson* (New York: Penguin Books, 1975).

Swami Prabhavananda, The *Spiritual Heritage of India* (Hollywood: Vedanta Press, 1980).

Hastings Rashdall, *The Theory of Good and Evil* (Oxford: Clarendon Press, 1907). Two volumes.

Robert D. Richardson, ed., *Emerson: Collected Essays, Lectures, and Poems* (New York: Bantam Books, 1990).

Peyton E. Richter and Walter L. Fogg, eds., *Philosophy Looks to the Future* (Prospect Heights, Illinois: Waveland Press, 1978).

Bertrand Russell, *Why I Am Not a Christian* (New York: Simon and Schuster, 1957).

Jean-Paul Sartre, *Existentialism* (New York: Philosophical Library, 1947).

Huston Smith, *The World's Religions* (San Francisco: HarperCollins, 1991).

Dennis Tamburello, *Ordinary Mysticism* (New York: Paulist Press, 1996).

Clarence D. Thorpe, *The Mind of John Keats* (New York: Oxford University Press, 1926).

Brian Tierney, Donald Kagan, and L. Pearce Williams, eds., *Great Issues in Western Civilization* (New York: McGraw-Hill, Inc., 1992).

Leo Tolstoy, *A Confession*. Trans. Aylmer Maude (London: Oxford University Press, 1974).

________, *The Death of Ivan Ilych*. Trans. Aylmer Maude (New York: Signet Books, 1960).

G. N. M. Tyrrell, *The Personality of Man* (Middlesex: Penguin Books, 1947).

Brenda Ueland, *If You Want to Write* (St. Paul, Minnesota: Graywolf Press, 1987).

Miguel de Unamuno, *The Tragic Sense of Life*. Trans. J. Crawford Flitch (New York: Dover Books, 1954).

Evelyn Underhill, *Mysticism* (New York: New American Library, 1974).

Index

Principal Names

A

B

C

D

E

F

G

H

J

K

R

S

T

U

V

W

Key Subjects

A

B

C

D

E

F

G

L

M

N

O

P

R

S

V

W

Z

To order additional copies of this book, or other books written by the author, please notify Homeward Bound Publishing, Inc. Place your order via phone, fax, mail, or e-mail.

Toll Free: 1-888-433-1130

Fax: 801-816-1170

E-mail: homewardpb@aol.com

Website: www.need2read.com

The cost of this book per copy is $19.95, plus $5.00 for shipping and handling. We accept most credit cards. You may also send check or money order to:

Homeward Bound Publishing, Inc.
Post Office Box 1468
499 East Parowan Way
Draper, Utah 84020

About the author:

Kelly Nicholson is an adventurer who approaches life and philosophy in an open-endedly spiritual fashion. A seasoned instructor of ethics, logic, and world religion, he has lived and taught in China, Wales, and the Slovak Republic, as well as in Utah and his native Pacific Northwest.

Kelly received his Ph. D. in philosophy from the Claremont Graduate School in 1989. He is the author of two additional works on philosophy entitled *The Prospect of Immortality* and *Body and Soul: The Transcendence of Materialism*.

During his college years, Kelly was a firefighter out of the Mt. Hood National Forest. A former amateur boxer, he has also written articles for *Ring* and *Boxing Illustrated* magazines while covering fight action in the Northwest arenas. He is a longtime sports fan who delights in baseball action and memorabilia. At present he resides in the state of Utah.